Folktales from Syria

Modern Middle East
Literatures in Translation Series

Folktales from Syria

Collected by Samir Tahhan

English Version and Introduction
by Andrea Rugh

Center for Middle Eastern Studies
The University of Texas at Austin

Library of Congress Catalogue Card Number: 2004113928
ISBN: 0-292-70630-8

Printed in the United States of America

Originally published in *Hakawti al-Halabi* (Beirut, 1980) and *Qisas al-Halabi* (Aleppo, 1982).

Partial funding for this publication awarded by the National Endowment for the Arts

Contents

Preface

While living in Syria in the early 1980s, I accepted the urgings of a friend to meet a remarkable young poet, Samir Tahhan. Though my friend had forewarned me of the dreadful accident that had befallen Samir, I was not prepared, upon meeting him, for the full implication of handicaps as devastating as his. In 1970, while serving in the Syrian military, a mine exploded, which severed his arms below the elbows, destroyed his hearing, blinded him completely in one eye, and eventually caused him to lose sight in the other eye. A series of operations failed to restore his sight, but others succeeded in restoring partial hearing. For a human being as dependent on his sense of hearing as Samir, this one partial recovery must have seemed a reprieve from a life of complete isolation.

The next happy event in Samir's life was an accidental meeting with a beautiful, serene young woman named Muna, who became his wife. Muna became the hands and sight he no longer possessed, making it possible for him to continue with his literary career. With her help, he published a book of Arabic poetry, a book of Spanish poetry written when Samir was convalescing in a Spanish hospital, two books of folk narratives translated into English in this volume, and a book of popular Arabic songs. In addition, a book of Samir's paintings, which were completed when he still had partial vision, was published in conjunction with a joint exhibition of his works at the British and French Cultural Centers in Damascus.

I must confess that in talking to Samir and Muna, I became infected with their enthusiasm for preserving some of the oral narratives that they feared would be lost after this generation of Syrian grandparents was gone. Altogether, Samir collected over sixty popular children's stories and tales. Ten stories and ten tales were published in two volumes in classical Arabic, so that children all over the Middle East and

North Africa might enjoy them. It is these two volumes that are translated here. The first book, *Hakawti al-Halabi,* (The Aleppo Storyteller) contains ten folktales collected from visits to professional storytellers and elderly people who still remember the tales. Several of these tales in the Arabic publication appear in rhyming verse, which, according to Samir, was a later adaptation. The second book, *Qisas al-Halabi,* (Stories of Aleppo) includes ten folk stories based on events that are said to have actually taken place in Aleppo.

Samir collected the narratives by going himself to listen and record the stories told by amateur and professional storytellers. Muna then transcribed and edited the tape. The collection of folk narratives was not, therefore, systematically or exhaustively collected as a folkloric scholar might have wanted to do it. The samples also are not meticulously catalogued by type of narrator or context in which the narration took place. Nor are they thoroughly analyzed for symbolic content. Nevertheless, the collection provides an example of three of the most popular types of Syrian folk narrative: the *qissa* or story, the *hikaya* or tale, and the *hudutha* or episode. The introduction explains in general terms some of the characteristics of these three forms for those who are interested. Mainly, however, the intent of the book is to provide an English speaking audience with the opportunity to become acquainted with a set of entertaining Syrian folk narratives.

In producing an English translation of an Arabic text, it has become my custom to work closely with a native speaker. In this way, the intricacies and double meanings of the Arabic language are less likely to interfere with the intended meanings. I want to express my gratitude to Lamia Keylani and Leila Martin who produced the first rough translations into English. I am responsible for the final English version and any errors that may have crept into the text or into the transliteration of Arabic into English.

I also want to acknowledge and express my appreciation for the illustrations provided by my son Douglas Rugh. Because he has the eye of an artist and because he grew up in the Middle East, he is well-

prepared to give an authentic and sympathetic picture of these imaginary happenings.

And, last, it is Samir's wish to dedicate this project to Joesph Pounds, his teacher whom he remembers so fondly.

Andrea Rugh
Sanaa 1986

Introduction

"Kan ya makan fi qadim al-ziman" are words as familiar to a Syrian child as the words, "Once upon a time," are to an American child. The two phrases are laden with the magic of anticipation for a story as yet unheard or with the delight of recognition in retold tales.

At least four distinguishable types of folk narrative are found in Syria; three are represented in this volume. They are the *qissa* or story, the *hikaya* or tale, and the *hudutha* or episode,[1] all designed for narrating in private homes or in other small gatherings. The fourth, the romance, the reader can find illustrated in the already translated[2] *'Antar and 'Abla*, which is roughly comparable to the English epic "Beowulf." In it, 'Antar, the son of a slave woman, and depicted always with a dark skin, falls in love with his paternal cousin, the beautiful, fair-skinned 'Abla. 'Abla's father is reluctant to allow her to marry 'Antar because of his slave mother's lowly origins, even though paternal-cousin marriage is the preferred form of marriage in many areas in the Arab world. Audience response to the epic romance reflects the widespread enthusiasm that existed before the advent of television. In contrast with other types of short folk narrative, romances were related in formal settings of coffee houses and large social gatherings. Their episodes continued over long periods of time through a number of installments. The storytellers, called *Hakawati,* knew by heart the basic elements of the long epics that were said to be originally based on true stories. Though the origins of the epics are not completely clear, they most probably began as descriptive stories and only later developed more complicated plots and, sometimes, even stable rhyming versions. Although the true events upon which they were based could have been related in the period of half an hour, the *Hakawati* could elaborate them with embellishments into a thousand hours. In the process, the storyteller would draw upon as much of the popular local knowledge and wisdom as he could to make the occurrences more appealing and relevant to his audience.

Because the stories were conveyed from mouth to mouth and not written down until later, early storytellers had a great deal of leeway in how they related the major episodes in the life of 'Antar and 'Abla. It was common in the cafes where the stories were told for factions to form, with patrons in support of certain characters cheering their favorites on one side and those opposed booing on the other. It was customary also for the listeners to bribe the storyteller to change the details of the episode to favor their own side. The storyteller would sit on a low bench (*mastabaa*) in the middle of his audience, sometimes elevated on a platform, holding his *rababa*, a single-stringed instrument that was used to accompany the musical parts of the romance. Usually, the owner of the cafe, who paid the basic price for the services of the storyteller, would hover near him, seeing to the needs of the customers and subduing the quarrels of the competing sides, should they threaten to erupt and damage his establishment. If the patrons became too heated, the cafe owner would put a stop to the storytelling for the evening or might beg the storyteller to bring the episode to a compromise conclusion so as not to incite the passions of the crowd.

The episodes of the romance sometimes would serve a subtle purpose in the local setting where the sides taken by patrons might reflect deep rifts in the community's equanimity. Not infrequently, the underlying enmity would become sublimated in the epic's events. In such cases, if a community dispute centered around property, for example, the storyteller might take the opportunity through the actions of his characters to advise the factions on the benefits of compromise or, more specifically, on the virtues of one solution over another.

'Antar, of course, would win major battles as well as victories in the individual episodes. One of the lessons the 'Antar and 'Abla epic teaches is contradictory to the generally held value that a person must take the side of other family members even when they are wrong. 'Antar takes the view that right is right even when it means opposing the rest of the family.

With the advent of television and, incidentally, the much beloved modern serialized dramas that last through many episodes of the lives

and loves of fictionalized characters, the popularity of the epic romances has diminished. Now they are rarely heard except under the auspices of the Minister of Culture during the evenings of Ramadan. The old battles of 'Antar and the wars between the Crusaders and the great Arab hero Salah al-Din are not as engrossing anymore as modern battles in Lebanon or events concerned with the Palestinians, nor are the romantic episodes as relevant to modern day audiences as the problematic loves of television heroes and heroines.

The folk narratives published here, in contrast to the epic romances, are short, self-contained, and designed for telling in smaller, more intimate gatherings. They are still familiar (or at least narratives like them are familiar) to many modern Syrians, perhaps because they have been related and preserved through the generations by family members and are shorter and more easily remembered. Among other functions, they continue to serve the need that the older generation has to hand down its social values to the upcoming generations.

The first group of folk narratives, in the form of stories (*gisas*), Samir Tahhan collected mainly from the old men in Aleppo who used to sit outside their houses, drinking tea and discussing the activities of the neighborhood that took place before their eyes. Some of these storytellers would come to be thought of as possessing a special wisdom (*hikma* or *fahm*), and people would consult them when they needed advice. Perhaps a parent would inform the sage of an inappropriate marriage a grown child wished to contract, and while the child was present the sage might tell a story about the consequences of such actions. He might create a story on the spot, or he might select something pertinent to the problem at hand from a set repertoire of known stories. The warning would be clear: that it is risky to marry out of one's class and social level. Then again in another such story a difference in rank would not be a significant impediment to marriage with even a prince. Stories, like popular aphorisms do not need to be mutually consistent. Each depends for its impact on the context in which it is told and the receptivity of its audience to a specific message at the time of its telling.

Folktales from Syria

The stories will appear familiar to a Western audience both in form and in the general content they express. Like Western fairy tales, their purpose on the most explicit level is didactic—that is, to teach lessons in morality and social values or simply to inform about the ways of the world. The stories are presented as serious narratives that are true enough to life so that they might have happened without resort to miraculous or super-human intervention. In general, this approach means that the actors are human, or, if animals are the main characters, that they behave in a way consistent with reality; that is, they don't talk or otherwise behave as human beings. One exception appearing in the text is "The Story of Luck and Fate," where a talking panther briefly appears at the end of the story. When Samir challenged his grandfather on this point, his grandfather responded that it was not the animal speaking of its own volition but rather an animal being used in the story as a vehicle for the words of God.

A clue to the origin of some of the stories lies in allusions to identifiably Christian or Muslim themes. Aleppo is a town with large communities of Muslims and various sects of Christians. A discerning Syrian reader can usually make an educated guess about which religious community a particular story originally came from. However, once a story becomes a part of the lore, it is no longer important whether a Muslim or a Christian tells the story, since each narrator is quite likely to add his or her own embellishments.

Syrians as a people are generally tolerant of different religious groups, and it is unlikely that people generate certain themes to promote their religious beliefs. Instead, those who first tell the stories tend to use the symbols and details with which they are most familiar. Therefore, rather than identify the stories positively as originating in one religious community or the other, which may prove inaccurate, let me review in general the details that a Syrian might use as markers. Normally, Christian stories would not mention divorce, polygamy, or revenge conflicts. They would be more likely to mention priests and holy symbols such as crosses and churches. Muslim stories tend to be peopled with sheikhs and Bedouin, and fateful incidents may occur that are not

4

Folktales from Syria

a direct consequence of the actions of the characters, as seen for example in "The Story of the Saintly Thief."

Muslim stories are more apt to divide the world of men and women clearly, as, for example, when a character enters the woman's quarters or joins the men in their reception rooms. A character's occupation is one important way of identifying religious origin, since the different religious communities in the past tended to monopolize certain of the trades.

Christians generally pursued craft and manual occupations that were frowned upon by Muslims. Thus stonecutters, peddlers, goldsmiths, gardeners, and weavers appearing in the stories are probably Christian, while Muslims tend to be occupied in government and commercial professions. Many of these distinctions have broken down now, but at the time these stories emerged, significant differences still existed. In attempting to identify the religious origins of the stories it is important to look at the markers in context. A single symbol alone may not be definitive.

The second form of narrative found in this book is the tale (*hikaya*), which is generally a nonserious, humorous entertainment, sometimes appearing in rhyming verse and designed for young children. Though the tales often convey moral messages, the meanings may be less profound than those in the more serious philosophical stories.

Most families in the past had their taletellers, often a grandfather or more likely a grandmother who because of old age was released from many of the daily responsibilities of the household. It was the delight of these older people to assume some of the care of the young children of the household. A harassed mother, constantly interrupted in her work by the distraction of her child, might say, "Go to your grandmother and tell her to 'tie the sheep' or 'hold with molasses' or 'the beans and remaining'," all phrases that in the secret language between mother and grandmother meant that the grandmother should keep the child occupied and out of the presence of the mother.

The grandmother would begin first with a rhyme that would distract the child and involve his or her participation. "Let's give an apple

and a ball to father, to mother, to little brother. And who do you want to give the apple and the ball to?" And the child's selections would be incorporated in the rhyming phrases. The repetition of the phrases helped the child learn Arabic sounds and increase vocabulary. A rhyme might start, "Selma went to the store and bought a sweet," and the child would repeat the phrase. Then the rhyme continued, "Selma went to the store and bought a sweet which she put in her pocket." With each repetition a new phrase would be added until there was a very long sentence that the child had to repeat. The challenge of completing the sentence in one breath would make the boredom of repeating the phrases fun for the child. Another participation game might involve role playing where the grandmother would play the part of a judge and the child would take the part of a petitioner.

The purpose of the *hikaya* was therefore first to amuse and distract, second to teach lessons in language, morality, and role-playing, or to make simple discriminations without the conscious knowledge of the child. The stories often involved animals that talked and so were explicitly imaginary. The use of animal actors served also to shield the children from too close an identification with the main characters, which might prove too intense in the case of fearsome or dangerous events.

The third form of narrative (*hadutha*), here called an episode to distinguish it from the stories and tales, appears in two examples: "TheEpisode of the Spilled Molasses" and "The Episode of the Mother Goat." Some analysts[3] consider the *hikaya* and *hudutha* to be essentially the same narrative form. Samir, however, sees the episode as a combination form. While it can usually be classified as a nonserious narrative, it may not fall exclusively into that category. For example, the episode may combine events based on reality with those that have a miraculous quality about them, as in "The Episode of the Spilled Molasses." Alternatively, an episode may combine a serious story line with imaginary animal characters as in "The Episode of the Mother Goat." It is not always easy to make categorical distinctions.

The folk tales translated here are only a drop in a rich and varied reservoir of Syrian folklore. They do not include, for example, prov-

erbs, jokes, lullabies, love poetry, or songs for special occasions such as weddings. Nor do the tales include stories about the nights of the fasting month of Ramadan and special Christian and Islamic feasts, or children's' street chants, or what must be clearly classed as folklore—the chants of peddlers passing through the streets of Aleppo. Moreover, they do not include the impromptu verses that poets hurl in challenge at each other in cafes or sometimes on television, where a verse started by one must be completed by another, in rhyme. It is often even difficult to separate narrative and music, since one is so much like another when rendered by Arabs in Arabic.

A listing of popular oral lore is not complete without mentioning the colorful tradition of *karacuza* (shadow play), which provides popular social criticism and instruction to the grownups and children that attend to their stories. A final popular art form that also bears mention combines visual with auditory pleasure. Familiar from the childhood of most Syrian adults is the *sanduk al-dinya*, a covered box with peep holes into which the child looks after paying his "penny" (or in some cases a piece of fruit, some bread, cheese, or whatever a child can scavenge from his mother's kitchen). As the narrator winds his pictures from one roll to another he chants, "And now you see the Great Pyramids of Egypt, etc. etc," exciting the imagination of the viewer with "believe-it-or-not" style commentary.

We have said that the narratives are didactic, whether as serious instruments of moral instruction or as merry tales teaching language, numbers, animal sounds, customs, and general information. The list is potentially endless. The child may not grasp the full meaning the first time he or she listens to the narrative, but when the adult explains in simpler language and continuously repeats the account, eventually even sophisticated words come to be understood.

For general comprehension and instruction, these narratives are designed for mature children from at least age seven and up to adulthood. Yet younger children find amusement in the yarns, and older people find them useful illustrative examples of popular truths, following the common discursive pattern of explaining a point with a descriptive case.

Folktales from Syria

One often hears, "What I am saying is just like what happened to so and so," and the story is told with some embellishment. It is easy to see how such everyday stories could be made anonymous and embroidered even further to fit the conventions of folk narration.

It would be a naive person who didn't see the usefulness of innocent-sounding folk tales in making political points as well. With very little effort, the narratives can be construed, whether intended or not, as advising rulers on their obligations to their people, as commenting on unnecessarily harsh treatment of citizens, and even as criticizing super-power approaches to Middle East issues without fully comprehending their complexity. Syrian adults enjoy drawing such parallels from the innocuous-seeming prose.

The narratives are thus enjoyed by people of all ages, providing within a flexible medium an instrument that offers something to everyone who listens. As the child grows, he or she learns to strip the "onion" of its ever-deeper layers of meaning, with each layer bringing its own kind of enjoyment. And simultaneously, the older person finds an enjoyment in the meanings attuned to his or her comprehension level, as well as enjoyment in the pleasures of the narration itself. My favorite example of this multi-layered phenomenon is a popular lullaby sung by mothers:

Sleep, my son, sleep
I'll kill a dove for you
Oh dove, don't believe what I say
I only tell lies so he will sleep

As a lullaby, the rhythm and melody are technically enough to soothe the child, but the popular version is not content with the single purpose of putting a baby to sleep. It reassures the older, comprehending child not to worry about the possibility of an early demise for the dove and slyly acknowledges in the presence of other adults the conspiracies of parents in achieving their purposes with children. As a whole the lullaby

expresses at the same time the sincere tenderness a mother feels for her child.

The explicit lessons to be learned from the narratives are the accepted social values and behaviors that adults wish to inculcate in the younger generation. From the stories we learn, for example, that it is desirable for people to share what they have, to be generous without expectation of return, to be modest and not overly proud, to treat others as you would expect to be treated, to be wise in your approach to problems, and to seize opportunities when they are presented or it may be too late. In addition, we learn the auxiliary lessons that a person's nature never changes, that bad behavior brings bad results, that people usually deserve what they get, that wisdom is not necessarily a function of age or size, and that you can't avoid your fate.

That the lessons are sometimes subtle and complicated is clear from "The Story of Luck and Fate." The story illustrates, along with the main point, that man cannot escape his fate and two more subtle messages. First, once you have taken a certain path you cannot fail to accept the consequences of that action, and, second, once you have rejected an opportunity you cannot go back and claim it at a later time. This advice is far from the idea of a passive acceptance of fate often attributed to Arabs by Westerners. The reader is told to make active choices at each juncture, but in the end one should not complain if his choices have led him to an unhappy conclusion. "Don't cry over spilled milk," is a good English equivalent to the Arabic "nasibak" (it is your fate). in this case.

The tales and episodes teach many of the same lessons as the stories, but, if there is a difference, it is that the lessons in the tales are presented in a lighter manner and the message is usually not as profound. The tale prefers a smaller truth rather than an all-encompassing one. We learn that people should seek justice and the good of all, that it is cleverness and not size that counts, that one should behave moderately, that one should be careful of whom one trusts, that the greedy person loses in the end, that one should mind one's own business, that no one looks after your interests like a mother (a committed one), and that right

when backed with might will be victorious. As with the stories, the implicit lessons of the tales are limited only by the imagination of the listener.

A number of conventions and formulae are found in the narratives. Many are based on the didactic device of repetition. We have already mentioned how the constant repetition of the narratives themselves allows them to be absorbed quickly by all ages. The pattern of repeating an action with variations a number or times within the narrative itself serves the same function of engraving the moral point more distinctly on the mind of the listener, while it builds suspense for a resolution to the problems raised. If indeed a true event existed behind the story or tale, it has been embellished and made more congruent by setting it within this repetitive mold.

A common device in Arabic, as in English, is to present a point in three repetitious actions. For example, we see such a device used in the story about the miser who offers a porter three pieces of advice. The repetition may involve a set number of specified actions that must be accomplished to test the hero or heroine, or actions that must be imitated in order to achieve anticipated results, or simply actions that are repeated a number of times to emphasize the main point. In "The Tale of Our Lady Namlush," reaction to the news of her husband's death draws a sympathetic response again and again from a series of characters. Most show their sympathy with behavior the tale condones as being appropriately moderate in scale and eventually reversible. It is the contrast of the one immoderate response that allows the point to be made. The conclusion then goes on to explain why things went wrong and what could have been done differently to avoid the problem.

Another way of using repetition is found in "The Episode of the Spilled Molasses." First, the heroine behaves in an exemplary manner with happy results; but, when her sister emulates the exemplary behavior in anticipation of the same rewards, she is disappointed. The moral compares the two behaviors in this and similar narratives and points out why, because of some miscarriage of the action or a wrong motive, the rewards are not forthcoming.

Sometimes, repetition of events simply underlines a point being made. In "The Tale of Three Mice," for example, each mouse is clever in its own way at avoiding becoming the cat's meal. In "The Story of the Stone Cutters and the Son of the Gardener," repeated absurdities bring down an appropriate consequence. A final repetition in these and other narratives brings home the point again. While the body of the text makes the point in the concrete form of an example, the statement of the moral repeats the point again in abstract philosophical terms. Thus, the listener absorbs the lesson at whatever level he or she finds most convenient.

Repetitive behavior internal to a narration is a pattern more common to the tales than to the stories. Tales, therefore, can more legitimately be referred to as formula narratives. By contrast, stories usually rely more heavily on the details of the person's character or actions rather that the repetitious acts of various actors for their impact. For this reason, both plots and actors are carefully elaborated. In "The Story of Master Karshush's Tarbush," for example, the narrator carefully sets the scene of the action and the special flaws in the character of Master Kartush that make the surprise ending plausible. Usually, the possession of some specific trait, such as miserliness, wisdom, stupidity, generosity, or excessive pride, allows the moral to be drawn.

Other commonly occurring formulae are found at the beginning and end of stories and tales. I have already noted the introductory rhyming phrase that is roughly equivalent to our "once upon a time."[4] Stories and tales, however, may also begin with such phrases as, "There was a place, my noble listeners," or "It happened one day that." Or, in some cases, the story begins immediately without a special phrase.

The introductory phrases for stories and tales show basically the same variation in this collection. However, in the two cases that are defined by Samir as episodes (haduth), the narration starts uniquely with, "I heard from Taq bin al-Tarintaq," an imaginary character who is supposed to have originated these particular episodes. His name conveniently rhymes widely with other words in preliminary phrases that have nothing to do with the basic story line that develops. Such openings are

designed primarily as a means of setting the mood by means of a brief round of rhythmic verses. The verses can be equated with our, "I'll tell you a story of Jack and McGory, and now my story's begun. I'll tell you another of Jack and his brother, and now my story is done." The meaning is subservient to the luscious feel of the words rolling off the tongue.

Ending formulae for stories, tales, and episodes are more stable than introductory phrases. Each type of narrative has its own convention that is determined by the need to find words that rhyme with the Arabic name for the type of narrative: *qissa*, *hikaya* or *hadutha*. For stories, the ending goes "Hissa, hissa, antahat al-qissa, be farha am bi ghussa," with not only an introductory word *hissa* that rhymes with *qissa* but also a final word *ghussa*. Literally the phrase translates as "Thus ends the story with its allotted share of joy and agony." In the text, an attempt to preserve some of the rhyme has resulted in a freer translation of, "Thus ends the story, with its share of grief and glory."

The tale also has its consistent ending, "Aya, aya, antahat al-hidaya, bi sha'a am halawiya." Literally this phrase translates, "Aya, aya (nonsense words), thus ends the tale, was it disgusting or entertaining?" In the text, the translation becomes a freer, "So that is the tale's ending, did you find it charming or offending?" The storyteller may demand an answer from the child telling whether he or she liked the tale or not. The child who answers hastily, "Oh, I liked it," is told, "Good, then you are satisfied, so go to sleep!" Next time, in hopes of hearing more tales, the child says, "No, I didn't like it. Tell me another one." The storyteller replies, "So my tales don't satisfy you, then I won't tell you anymore. Go to sleep!" The joke is understood by the child and the storyteller, who both know that victory in the struggle of wits lies with the storyteller.

The final ending formula that appears in this collection is the one specifically designed for the *hudutha*, "Tuta, tuta, antahat al-hadutha, marbuta am mafluta?"[5] Literally, this phrase translates as "Tuta, tuta (nonsense words) so ends the episode, all tied up (complete) or with loose ends (inconclusive)?" In the text the freer translation reads, "Thus the episode ends with all its events, was it unclear or did it make sense?"

All the ending formulae bridge the gap between formal narration and normal conversation by engaging the listener in comments about the presentation.

Preceding the ending formula in one story appearing here is another familiar conclusionary phrase that is roughly equivalent to the English, "And they lived happily ever after." In "The Story of the Peddler's Daughter," after the resolution of the problem issue, the narrative continues, "And so one year succeeded another, and she bore boys and girls and they all lived healthy and strong until the day came when the one who destroys all pleasure and dispatches all groups appeared and demanded their souls, and thus they died." More than the English equivalent, this ending specifically names what people can expect from life: children as the source of pleasure, and death as an inevitable end that comes even to princesses and princes.

It is interesting that the endings in these narratives all develop a properly rising crescendo of tension and a definite climax as the suspense is resolved, similar to a Western folk narrative. In this, the narratives differ from what is more typical in Arabic art, music, and literature: the never-ending sequence of roughly equivalent events or episodes. We find examples in the interminable saga of "The Thousand and One Nights," in geometric Islamic motifs where angles of equal weight leave no single point for the eye's attention, and in the hours-long songs of the famous singer Um Kalthum. The audience finds itself back at the beginning when an artistic piece is ended, in an episodic cycle of beginnings and endings much more true to the reality of life. With a moral point very much in focus, however, the narratives take a different course, building toward their goal and ceasing when the point is made.

These narratives differ from the usual Arabic literary tradition in yet another way. In general, Arabic prefers an elaborate, embellished plot, replete with florid descriptive passages. But, instead, the narratives appearing here are usually composed in a spare, restrained style that outlines only the critical elements of the plot. They jump time and distance without describing more than briefly what transpired in the

interim. They usually pause only briefly to highlight significant details that describe settings, what people were thinking or doing, and how they reacted to unexpected events. One can be sure, however, that every detail is relevant in some way to the story's conclusion. In "The Story of the Merchant of Khan al-Wazir," for example, the narrative describes the types of people who make up the audience coming to watch the execution of the debt agreement: the gloaters, condolers, sympathizers, and those who rejoice in the misfortune of others. The important point is that everyone responds emotionally to the impending tragedy but no one is ready to provide what is necessary to prevent it. In the story "The Miser and the Porter," the storyline is even more restrained with the narrative moving quickly to essential actions, as the pragmatic porter, trying to make the best of a bad situation, accepts advice instead of money. The long, steep stairway up which he carries his burden suggests the difficulty of his task and the appropriateness of his revenge when he realizes how badly he has been taken in. No extra words are needed to convey his feelings.

Detail is used only when the plot requires elaboration of a point to make a conclusion more plausible. The young girl in "The Story of the Peddler's Daughter" must be described at length to convince the listeners that someone so immature might possess the cleverness to fool the authorities as she does. In general, keeping the storyline clear and uncomplicated is most certainly an orientation dictated by the comprehension level of the youthful audience with its short attention span and need for a simple, logical sequence of events to grasp the main moral point. By contrast, epic romances designed primarily for adult listeners can afford the elaborate, flamboyant plots with intricate digressions beloved by Arab audiences.

The English language falls far short in conveying the sounds, rhythms, and emotions of the Arabic language. When English remains objective, Arabic is subjective. When English describes minimally, Arabic may be redundant with reiterations of the same word or synonyms. The young woman who doesn't eat is not just in danger of being ill; she is also pale, weak, and thin. When English is impersonal, Arabic ap-

peals to the emotions in a mist of phrases that tenderly or cruelly tug at the heartstrings. When English searches for preciseness in meaning, Arabic prefers to create a vague ambiguity with words that flow in musical instead of logical succession. Where English style requires short, direct, declarative sentences, Arabic loves the endless sentence strewn with past participles and past perfects and connected with "and," "or," and "but," as if releasing the eye with a period might forever lose the attention of a distracted reader. Arabic abhors the uninvolved, the impersonal, and the uncommitted, and with its poetic oratory strives to envelop its reader in the gossamer strands of raw sentimentality.

The *hikaya* tales by the nature of their rhymes, nonsense words, and sometime pointless maneuvers to set the mood are much more difficult than stories to translate satisfactorily into English. The importance of their rhythms, didactic repetitions, and participatory goals must be kept in mind when translations fall short of complete communication.

Andrea Rugh

[1] I have chosen to represent the different narrative forms with these English equivalents to avoid confusion.

[2] See 1978, *'Antar and 'Abla: A Bedouin Romance*, Quartet Books Ltd., London.

[3] See El-Shamy, Hasan M., 1980, *Folktales of Egypt*. University of Chicago Press. Chicago. p.xlv.

[4] "Kan ya makan fi gadim al-zaman" means literally "There was a place in olden times."

[5] El-Shami says that this ending and those similar to "and they begat boys and girls" are phrases used more frequently by women and children in Egypt. Samir notes that he collected the *gisas* primarily from old men and notes the greater involvement of women in relating the less serious *hikaya* and *hudutha*. This observation would be consistent therefore with El-Shamy's comments, but more as a matter of who relates a particular type of narrative rather than as a matter of the ending itself.

Part One
Stories of Aleppo

The Story of the Beggar Queen

ONCE UPON A TIME in a bygone era, there was a king (but there is, of course, no king except God). He was like an omnipotent shah in whom was entrusted all worldly power and prestige. This king was a good king who tried with all his might to protect his people from pain and unhappiness. Every night, he would disguise himself as a poor beggar so he could go into the town and learn how his people lived and come to know their problems first hand.

One time in his nightly rambles, the king met a young beggar girl who was alone in the world without relatives or acquaintances. He was attracted to her and urged her to come travel with him around the country, begging in her usual fashion. His friendship for her turned into love, and his love into a passion that determined him to marry her and declare her queen of the whole kingdom.

He thus proclaimed a period of celebration and feasting that would last forty days and forty nights. During that time, no one should eat or drink except at the table of the king. In a wedding ceremony, the likes of which people had never seen before, the beautiful young beggar girl became his bride.

Hardly a week had passed, when the king became worried and preoccupied. His face showed signs of fatigue and anxiety, as if something

serious was bothering him. One pleasant evening of the kind where it is nice to sit up late and chat, the king and his companion were sitting in the garden of the palace conversing and drinking wine. Suddenly, the king became distracted, as if with a problem that was impossible to solve.

When his friend noticed the change in the king, he became concerned and said, "I would give my life for you, O Mighty King! Why are you so distracted, sitting there with your head in your hands that way? Do you have news that a ship has sunk, or do you suffer from an unrequited love?"

Looking into the eyes of his friend, the king answered, "O good friend, you who know every little thing that happens in this kingdom, I am perplexed by a problem for which I have no explanation. Since I married the queen, she has taken neither food nor drink from what is put before us on the table. When we are through, she has not touched a single morsel. For that reason, I am terribly afraid she may become weak and die."

His friend thought for awhile and then said, "In truth, O Eternal King, I don't remember seeing in any of the books I have read about the saints and prophets whose souls were filled with God's spirit and whose eyes were filled with God's light, or in what I have read about mystics and hermits who care not for worldly possessions, that any one of them, no matter how little they ate, went without a single bite of food or drop of water. This by God, is most unusual, something I have never heard of before."

The king sighed and said, "This is the problem. How would you explain it, my good friend?"

The friend knelt in front of the king and bowed his head, touching the king's robe. "Promise me I will not be harmed, O Eternal King, you who possess the power of protection and peace."

"Say what you will. Have no fear."

The friend lowered his eyes and asked hesitantly, "Does the queen perform her natural functions to your knowledge, O King?"

"As far as I know, she does, like all other creatures both human and animal on the face of the earth."

The king gave a sigh of relief and thanked his friend for his advice. He rose to go to bed and sleep now that his mind was relieved of its worries. Next morning, the king pretended to go to work in the throne room as was his habit every day, but instead of going there he made his way to the servants' quarters. There, he disguised himself as a servant and set out to watch every move and gesture of the queen. From a hiding place, he saw her furtively slip into the pantry and take out dishes of food and bottles of drink. She set them on the windowsill and then she reached out her left hand with the palm up, in the manner she used when begging. Next, with her right hand she placed food and drink in her left hand as someone might do if he were giving alms to another. In this way, she ate until she was filled. She returned everything carefully to its place and left. The king came out of his hiding place smiling with joy. He took off his disguise and returned to his normal apparel, contented, with his soul at ease and his mind at rest. He called his friend to tell him what he had seen.

The friend nodded his head and said, "Now I understand what the ancients meant when they said, "Your nature never changes until you are buried in your grave."

Thus ends the story, with its share of grief and glory!

The Story of the Five Cakes

ONCE UPON A TIME, there was a poor widow with five children. She loved them as the earth loves the seeds, and they loved her as the seeds love the rain. One night when there was no food left to give her children except five cakes, she went and prepared some tea. She brought the tea and distributed the five cakes so that each child could have one cake. Then she sat quietly drinking her tea with no food left for herself.

The oldest of the children looked at his mother and thought, "My poor mother! She divided all the cakes she had among us and left none for herself to fill her empty stomach. God knows how much she has worked for our sakes, washing clothes, cleaning, ironing, shopping, cooking, washing dishes, sewing, and all the other tiresome chores. I

must share my part with her." Immediately, he divided his cake into two, giving one to his mother and keeping one for himself. When the next son saw what his brother had done, he presented his mother with his second half and so did the third and fourth and fifth sons, so that their mother found two and one-half cakes placed in front of her. The mother looked at her children with a smile and said, "Look what has happened, when one makes little sacrifices, one is compensated with a lot. You see what has happened to me. I had nothing to begin with and now I have more than any one of you." She put out her hand and took one-half a cake like her children and put the remaining two cakes in the middle of the table, so if anyone felt the desire to have more he could help himself a second time.

So all of them were satisfied and slept happily, enjoying love and affection, which is more valuable than any wealth, and sufficient compensation for any need or lack. Keep yourselves from calamity and evil. Learn that in selfishness there is dishonor, and that the road to greatness is through giving.

Thus ends the story, with its share of grief and glory!

The Story of the Merchant of Khan al-Wazir[1]

ONCE UPON A TIME, one of the honorable merchants of Khan al-Wazir faced a financial crisis which obliged him to seek a loan to solve his problems and start afresh. After a great deal of effort searching far and near, he came upon a petty moneylender. The man agreed to lend him what he needed on condition that he return the money on a certain day at a certain hour. If the merchant was late by even one minute of the fixed time, the money lender would have the right to chop off his hand. There would be no going back on the agreement, nor would it be subject to repeal or higher appeal. Since the merchant had no other alternative, being as he was so badly in need of money, he agreed to the proposal under duress, even though the conditions were exceedingly harsh. He signed a legal note to that effect in front of a notary.

The poor merchant worked very hard, trying his best to gather the amount of money he owed. But the agreed-upon day and hour were soon upon him before he had the chance to accumulate enough money to pay back the loan. He ran swiftly from door to door, knocking at the homes of relatives, friends, friends of friends, companions, and acquaintances, but everywhere his requests were rejected. They all made excuses and evaded his pleas. In the end he gave up, accepting his fate,

and in the final crucial moment sat surrounded by his crying children and his shrieking wife.

People gathered around him: the condolers, the gloaters, the rejoicers at misfortune, and the sympathizers. After a few minutes passed, the moneylender came to claim his debt, demanding that the articles of the contract be carried out minutely, one by one. The merchant, his family, and the bystanders tried hard to soften the heart of the money lender and postpone for a few days or even half a day the execution of the contract in hopes that after an hour or two something might happen to avoid the calamity. But the moneylender refused all their pleas, insisting stubbornly that the articles be carried out to the letter. The merchant and the people were powerless to change the moneylender's mind or curb his cruelty in carrying out the agreement. As everyone stood at a loss, the moneylender brought out his dagger and held it close to the hand of the merchant, who was trembling from head to foot with fear and dread.

Just as the blade was about to touch the merchant's skin, a stranger sprang from the crowd shouting, "Stop, put away your dagger, I am ready to pay this man's debts for him." He walked over to the petty moneylender and paid the sum to the last penny. Then he walked slowly to the merchant, who was faint from utter amazement, and said, "Keep this in mind, if it weren't for me you would be without a hand now." The merchant fell on the stranger, kissing his hand and saying, "I will be indebted to you for this good deed all my life. I will always remember you and will be grateful for your kindness. I will beg God to let me repay you, O noble and courageous man, O good and generous one. You are an angel come down from the sky...," and so on and so forth in words appropriate from someone who had experienced a great fright and then been delivered from it.

In this way the merchant was saved and the crowd dispersed. Everyone went home, telling about what they had seen. But the matter did not stop here. Rather it began. The next morning the stranger bought a shop next to that of the merchant in Khan al-Wazir. Every time he passed the merchant's shop he would enter and say, "You must re-

member that if it were not for me you would have no hand now." The merchant would answer with heartfelt words of gratitude and warm words of thanks for this deed. And so it went, day after day, week after week, month after month until it became intolerable.

Because his affairs were improving somewhat, the merchant thought to himself, "Maybe if I give him back the sum I owe, he will stop exaggerating my debt to him." So he set to work energetically day and night, night and day, until he gathered the whole amount and returned it to the stranger with his deepest thanks. But the stranger continued to increase his pattern of visiting the merchant to remind him of his good deed.

So the merchant said to himself, "Maybe if I buy him an appropriate present he will stop reminding me of my debt to him." He went out and bought an expensive gift and presented it to the stranger as a token of his gratitude. But every time the stranger met him, he continued to tell him "If it were not for me, you would be without a hand."

One day when the stranger came into the shop, as was his habit every time he passed in front of the door, he barely had time to open his mouth to repeat the words, when the merchant drew out a knife and cut off his own hand. He presented the hand to the stranger saying, "Please take this hand and leave me alone. By God, it is much better to live without a hand than to live without self-respect." Some customers were gathered around the shop and when they saw what happened they were shocked. But when they understood the reason, they said, "The merchant is right; even death is preferable to living always in debt. It is much better for a person who does a good deed to throw it in the sea, rather than to exact its price by demanding gratitude."

Thus ends the story, with its share of grief and glory!

[1] "Khan" is the Turkish word for *suq*, or place where goods are sold. This title means literally the Wazir's (Minister's) Suq.

The Story of the Miser
and the Porter

ONCE UPON A TIME, a miser went to the *suq* to buy some glassware. He proposed to a porter that he carry the purchase of glassware to his house for one quarter of a piaster and, because there was so little work, the porter agreed. The porter put the goods in his basket and hoisted them on his back as he followed in the footsteps of the miser.

Once they had gone a short way, the miser approached the porter and said, "What would you think if, instead of the fee, I gave you three pieces of advice that you could profit from all your life? I will give you the first one now, the second halfway along our route, and the third at the door of my house."

The porter answered, "By God, my master, I am a poor man who wants to live, and to live you need a home to shelter you, food for your stomach, and clothes for your back, These require money, not advice."

The miser said, "I don't doubt what you say is true, but remember there are sayings and advice that are more valuable than money."

The porter thought about this for a minute and said to himself, "Maybe this is a wise or learned man who has advice that would be beneficial to me. So I won't regret it later, I'd better accept his proposal. I can listen to his advice and forget the quarter of a piaster." He turned to the miser saying, "I agree to your proposal. Now, my master, let me hear the first piece of advice."

The miser said, "If someone tells you that the one who rides is like the one who walks, tell him he is wrong."

The porter said, "Good," and they continued walking. When they reached the halfway point along their road, the porter said, "Now we are halfway, my master, it is time for the second piece of advice."

The miser replied, "If someone tells you that the one who is tired is like the one who is rested, tell him he is mistaken."

The porter said "Good." They continued walking until they reached a steep staircase. When they came to the top and stopped at the door of the miser's house, the porter said, "It is time for the third piece of advice."

The miser said, "If someone tells you that the one who goes up is like the one who comes down, tell him he is wrong."

The porter said, "Good," and he took the basket from his back and hurled it as hard as he could down the flight of stairs. While it was rolling and bumping down the stairs, the porter turned to the miser and said, "If someone tells you that a single piece of glassware will remain whole and unbroken, tell him he is mistaken." And he grabbed up his basket and leapt down the stairs. While he was running away, he said, "It's true what they say, that the one who tries to cheat another with guile will find his own money squandered."

Seeing that his glassware was all scattered in pieces, the miser ran swiftly down the steps and knelt beside the remains to try to gather them together again. He shouted to the neighbors to stop the fleeing porter and repeated again and again, "Oh how times have changed! Before, advice was worth the price of a camel. Now, it is worth nothing but a catastrophe."

Thus ends the story, with its share of grief and glory!

The Story of Soaking the Bread

ONCE UPON A TIME, there was a woman who had a lazy husband. He was so lazy that he wouldn't even take his hand off his leg. He was so lazy that he needed someone to chew his food for him and put it in his mouth. One day this couple had nothing to eat except some dry bread, so dry that it was harder than stone and so old that it was impossible to bite without soaking it in water. The woman stood and said to him, "Come on you lazy man, start your blood moving. Put this bread in water to soak so we can have something to eat. I am so hungry and weary." Her husband replied with his usual slothfulness, "By God, I'm not able to do this; my head is hurting me and my eyes are burning, my throat is sore, my shoulders are weak, my hands are trembling, my back is aching, my breath is short, my stomach feels like nails, my intestines are colicky. I have no strength, my legs are numb and my feet swollen. Oh woman, don't you know that heavy blood like mine is a blessing because those with light blood have no substance?"

The woman answered with anger, "What have you got that is not sick? What are you capable of doing? You cold-hearted, lazy, unfeeling person. A dog's tail would sooner go straight than you change your slothful, stupid, and cynical ways." The husband answered back with

icy coldness, "What I possess is the capacity for true thinking, a logic that is not faulty, and plenty of tricks to get people to invite me to eat good food, drink well, and rest easily. So, be quiet, you woman! Don't throw a temper tantrum and be angry with me. Come, let us make a deal between us. The one who first opens his mouth to speak a word will be the one to soak the bread."

The woman said, "All right, this is a good solution and I accept." So they sat silently with their lips pressed together as second followed second, minute followed minute, and hour followed hour. It was a silence like the silence of the dead. The woman got bored from sitting so long, and her mouth became dry from lack of talk. She stood up and signaled to her husband that she was going for a short walk. But the husband remained in his corner with no movement whatsoever.

Suddenly, as he sat there alone, thieves came and stole everything in the house—furniture and everything—leaving it completely empty. The husband sat motionless with no sign of concern as if he were a statue. When the wife came back from her walk and found the house empty, she was so surprised she ran to her husband to ask what had happened. As soon as she opened her mouth to talk, her husband turned to her and said, "Stop where you are! You have spoken, so you must go soak the bread." The woman was furious and grabbed her husband by his throat to shake him, saying, "This is no time to be so bloody cold, you slob! Stop joking and tell me what happened." The husband said in his lethargic way, "Nothing at all, only some thieves came and stole everything. Don't change the subject. Go soak the bread."

The woman started beating her face and wailing, shouting, and crying and repeating over and over, "Why didn't you shout to stop them?" The husband, smiling like an all-knowing genius, answered, "Do you think I'm stupid enough to open my mouth and say a word so I would lose the bet and have to soak the bread?" The poor woman fell into the arms of the neighbors who came rushing to see what was wrong when they heard the shouting and screaming. She kept repeating, "There is nothing worse than impotence except stupidity, and there is no one as stupid as you, you silly soaker of bread!"

Thus ends the story, with its share of grief and glory!

The Story of the Stonecutters and the Gardener's Son

ONCE UPON A TIME, there were four stonecutters. They used to spend their weekends among the orchards and fields, far from city noises and busy streets. Their custom was to enjoy themselves with exercise and a change from the routine of working days.

One holiday they prepared food and drink and started out in the direction of the gardens of 'Ayn al-Tal outside Aleppo. When they reached their destination, they looked for a shady nook where they could avoid the hot rays of the sun. They found a beautiful tree where, by chance, among the thick leaves of its branches the son of the gardener was hiding. They spread their carpet beneath this tree, took out canteens, and settled down to chat and drink.

By the time they were finished with their first drink and before they had started on their next, the wine had already gone to their heads. They started encouraging each other to sing, but each one refused and it went back and forth this way until they began to get silly. To put an end to the discussion each one agreed to sing in turn.

While this was going on, the gardener's son in his hiding place was content to wait for the lovely tunes and beautiful poetry that he anticipated would be like a light to illuminate the dark night. After a lot of saying "yes" and "no," the stonecutters decided it should be Abu Yusef

who would start the singing because he was the oldest of them all. They made a circle around him and drank to his health, saying, "Come on, Abu Yusef, give us a beautiful song and let us hear from a mouth that is only capable of bringing forth jewels."

He cleared his throat and started to sing: "If my wife had done the washing, she would have washed the clothes. If she had not done the washing, she would not have washed the clothes."

After he finished this beautiful song, everyone began to praise him. Over the drinking and singing, one stonecutter said incredulously, "What is this tune that is lighter than a butterfly? By God, Abu Yusef, if the kings had heard you they would have made you king of them all, the king of arts and singing."

All the other stonecutters nodded their heads in agreement. One went on to say, "Be quiet you young men, listen, listen! Now it's the turn of Abu Jamil! Give us one of your beautiful tunes and make us sway in rhythm with your voice that is more polished than marble."

Abu Jamil, swaying and chanting, started to sing. "If my wife had done the ironing, she would have ironed the clothes. If she had not done the ironing, she would not have ironed the clothes." As soon as Abu Jamil finished his masterpiece all the other stonecutters greeted him with shouts of praise.

Over the drinking and shouting and cheering, one of them stood to say, "What is this beautiful song that makes the sane go mad and the mad go sane? By God, Abu Jamil, if the angels had heard you they would have worshiped you above all except for God. Oh, you angel from heaven!"

All the other stonecutters nodded their heads in agreement. One stood up to say, "Be quiet, fellows, now it's the turn of Abu Nayim. Come let us hear what you have to sing, Abu Nayim. Sing us something with your beautiful voice that makes the dead rise from their graves."

Abu Nayim cleared his throat and started humming and then began to sing. He sang, "If my wife cooked, she would have cooked a meal. If she had not cooked, she would not have cooked a meal."

When Abu Nayim was finished with his masterpiece, all the other stonecutters started to clap and whistle. One stood up and said with utter amazement, "What's this wonderful tune that makes the elderly turn young? By God, Abu Nayim, if the birds on the trees heard you, they would kill themselves or hurry to kneel at your feet, you lark of the East and nightingale of the West."

All the other stonecutters nodded their heads in agreement and some went on to say, "Now it's the turn of Abu Shukri. You, Abu Shukri, give us a dancing tune, you the singer of all singers!"

Abu Shukri hummed and started to sing. "If my wife washed, she would have washed the dishes. If she had not washed, she would not have washed the dishes."

As soon as Abu Shukri was finished with this pearl of a song, all the stonecutters threw themselves on the ground, drunk and still swaying with the rhythm. Then one of them stood up to say, "What is this beautiful dancing tune that achieves perfection? By God, Abu Shukri, if the skies heard you sing thus, they would have wept rain enough to satisfy the earth."

When the stonecutters reached this point, the gardener's son couldn't bear their silliness anymore and urinated on them. When they felt the urine on their heads like rain, they looked up and discovered the gardener's son hidden in the branches of the tree. They pulled him down and took him to the judge of the city to look into the matter. After some waiting, the judge called them and asked their problem.

One said, "Your Excellency, we are stone cutters who love to drink and sing in the midst of nature. So we went today to one of the orchards, 'Ayn al-Tal, and sat under a tree. We drank and sang, each by turn, and I was the first. I sang, 'If my wife had done the washing she would have washed the clothes. If she had not done the washing, she would not have washed the clothes.' My friends clapped and acclaimed me. If the kings had heard me, they would have made me king of the music and singing. Abu Jamil followed with the next turn and sang, 'If my wife had done the ironing, she would have ironed the clothes. If she had not done the ironing, she would not have ironed the clothes.'

We praised him and said that if the angels had heard him they would have worshiped him above all others except God, because his voice is so heavenly and angelic. Then came Abu Nayim next to sing, 'If my wife had cooked, she would have cooked a meal. If she had not cooked, she would not have cooked a meal.' We praised him and told him that if the birds in the trees had heard his singing they would have killed themselves or run to kneel at his feet to worship him. Abu Shukri's turn came next and he stood to sing, 'If my wife had washed, she would have washed the dishes. If she had not washed, she would not have washed the dishes.' We praised him and told him that if the skies were dry and heard him they would have wept enough rain to satisfy the earth. No sooner had we said this than we felt urine coming down like rain on our heads. We looked up and found the gardener's son hidden in the branches of the tree. We pulled him down and brought him to your Excellency to look into the matter."

The judge looked at the gardener's son and said "By God, you young fool, all you did was pee on them when you should have shat on them. He who composes and sings so badly must surely get as bad as he gives."

Thus ends the story, with its share of grief and glory!

The Story of Master Karshush's Tarbush[1]

ONCE UPON A TIME in the Khan Qaysariya in the Aleppo *suq*, there was a spinner who was very fond of the art of singing, so fond in fact that it became a kind of fascination for him. This spinner liked music and singing so much that he made it a rule that his workers could not speak in normal tones but should hum or sing their words in tunes. The spinner learned every tune and every way of singing, so people began to call him Master Karshush[2] from the fact that he knew all the tricks of the art of singing.

As it happened, one time Master Karshush had a worker with a beautiful voice, a good ear for music, and strong vocal cords, as well as experience in all the types of Arabic music. He was so good that he even surpassed the professionals in the art of singing, although he was but an amateur.

One day while Master Karshush and his workers were spinning silken threads, the worker started to sing a lovely dancing tune. In time to the tune, he sang, "Oh blessed be your hands, O Master. Give me the threads, if you please. Oh how lucky the one who learns from you, O Master. You are the best who ever taught or talked."

But Master Karshush interrupted, not able to resist showing off his knowledge of music. "This is not the way to sing. It is more like beating something. It is not artistic. You should sing the words this way and

that way and form the notes this way and that way...," and he went on and on explaining to him how to do it right.

The worker nodded his head, saying to Master Karshush, "This is a master speaking words worth a thousand normal comments, even though you may not be conscious of their true value. Your words, O Master of Masters, have the ring and the worth of gold pieces. From now on, I will never sing without following your instructions or without fully understanding the music."

Several days passed after this conversation took place, and Master Karshush and his worker were again spinning at their wheels. The worker began to sing, "O Ma-a-a-s-s-t-e-r...," slowly drawing out his words.

Master Karshush was swaying and keeping time with the music while he praised the worker, "O you, the best of all ages. You are the Zariab[3] of this age. You are the emperor of the art of singing."

The worker repeated the words of the tune, drawing them out as he had been told, "O my Master, O Friendly One... O my Master, O Friendly One, the truth..., O my Master, O Friendly One, the truth is..., O my Master, O Friendly One, the truth is that your..., O my Master, O Friendly One, the truth is that your tarbush..., O my Master, O Friendly One, the truth is that your tarbush is on fire!"

Master Karshush was not aware of the meaning of the song until it was finished and he awakened to reality. He ran to look at his tarbush, and was surprised to find that fire had turned it to ashes. Turning to the worker, he said, "O you idiot, couldn't you have sung the song in faster rhythm." The worker answered, "I am one who always listens to what my master tells me."

Beware of expert advice that is inflated with no substance or your end will be like that of Master Karshush's tarbush.

Thus ends the story, with its share of grief and glory!

[1] The tarbush is a red felt pillbox hat sometimes called fez. It is usually worn by those who are of a respectable station in life.

[2] The joker.

[3] A famous singer.

The Story of the Peddler's Daughter

ONCE UPON A TIME, my learned audience—I'm going to tell you a little folktale before you go to sleep—there was a king. But, of course, there is no kingdom except the Kingdom of Justice (he who is unjust, let him be sympathetic and fair). This king had issued an order, forbidding peddlers from calling out their wares on the streets. He would punish anyone who disobeyed his orders by sending him to prison for life.

Once it happened that a very poor peddler, who only barely survived from day to day by the fruit of his labor, was sentenced to prison. This peddler had a young daughter no more than ten years of age, a beautiful girl, more beautiful than the moon. There was no one as intelligent or bright as she was. In addition, she had a deep understanding of life and good sense. When this little girl heard about the misfortune of her father's imprisonment in a dark prison, she became angry and swore she would not rest nor let anyone else rest until she rescued her father from this unjust punishment.

She devised a plan to implement her decision and put it into action without delay. According to her plan, she went downtown and bought

a bra, a bride's transparent dancing dress, and some high heels, and returned home. She hennaed her hair, took a bath, and arranged her hair. She stuffed the bra with bits of rags and wool and put it on in a way that made her breasts stick out. She put on a shimmery dress and high-heeled shoes to make her look taller. Except for her tiny features, she could be taken for an eighteen- or twenty-year-old girl. She stood before her mirror to finish her toilette and then practiced her dancing steps until evening.

The little girl left the house and walked in the direction of the royal palace to join in a ball that was taking place there, as announced by the king that day. All the young marriageable women were to be present, so the king could choose a bride for his son, the young prince. When she reached the door of the palace and was about to enter, a guard stopped her and asked, "Where are you going, little one?"

She answered, "I'm going to take part in the ball, and, besides, I'm not so young, Mr. Guard!"

The guard became angry and said, "Go away, right now! You are much too young to take part in such a ball! Don't try to tell me you are not too young. I'm not so stupid that I can't tell the difference between those who are younger and those who are older. I mean it, go away voluntarily or I will use force on you!"

The peddler's daughter smiled and replied, "Take it easy, Mr. Guard, and don't be angry. Youth and age are not measured by the height of a person or by the width of the shoulders or the number of years. It is measured by the depth of intellect and deeds." She stooped and picked up a pebble, saying to the guard, "Look how little this pebble is, yet see what it can do." She threw the pebble in the opposite direction from the palace door. When the guard looked to see where it would go and what it would do, the little girl slipped into the garden that led to the ball. She entered, making sure she was safe from being sent away again. She pulled herself up to her full height, arranged her dress, and then joined the other women guests who were performing their dances one by one.

After some time, her turn came. She went to the floor and began her dance. Her movements were beautiful and graceful, accomplished

with dignity and pride and without vulgarity. She was so enchanting that she charmed everyone present. The young prince was almost driven mad by his admiration for her. As soon as she was finished with her dancing, the whole ball exploded with applause and shouts of appreciation. The king came down from his throne, accompanied by the prince, to congratulate her on the beauty of her dance.

When the little peddler's daughter saw the king standing before her, she fell on her knees and beseeched him, "Promise me I will not be harmed, O Mighty King!"

He touched her on the shoulder, "Don't be afraid. You are safe!"

The peddler's daughter said to the King, "O Mighty King, I have one question, which I want you to answer. Will you grant me permission to ask this one question?"

The king answered, "Ask any question you like. Don't be afraid or embarrassed."

The peddler's daughter stood up with assurance and dignity. With respect and politeness, she addressed the king in a clear voice with no sign of timidity, "What is the purpose of dancing, your Majesty?"

The king answered, "Dancing is an exercise that displays the qualities and the beauty of the one who performs it."

The peddler's daughter continued calmly with no sign of emotion or anger, "So you don't forbid people from dancing but, on the contrary, call on them to perform. Why did you forbid the peddlers and other salesmen from calling out their wares when all they were doing was drawing attention to the quality and beauty of their goods? What I want to ask is why you sent my poor father to jail for life a few hours ago simply because he was trying to call out the qualities of his wares and make them more appealing to his customers. O King, you have come down from your throne to congratulate me on my dancing. What is my dancing but a way of displaying the qualities I possess? Don't you know, O King—may God preserve your fame—that cutting off a person's head is better than cutting of his livelihood? Kings should make rules beneficial to their people rather than ones that are detrimental to them.

When the king heard the words of the peddler's daughter, he was struck by her intelligence as well as by her beauty. He issued an order that peddlers would be permitted to go through the streets calling out their wares, and he ordered that those who had been sentenced to prison should be set free. Later, the king gave the peddler and his daughter a suite in the palace and brought a multitude of wisemen and teachers to instruct her so that when she became of age, she would wed the young prince.

One year succeeded another and the king gave up his kingdom to his son, who married the peddler's daughter and proclaimed her queen. She bore him boys and girls, and they all lived, happy and strong, until the time when the one who destroys all pleasure and disperses all groups appeared before them. He said to the queen, "Give me your soul," and to the king, "Give me your soul," and thus they both died.

Thus ends the story, with its share of grief and glory!

The Story of the Saintly Thief

ONCE UPON A TIME, there was a king but, of course, there is no king but the King of Perfection. He who seeks perfection must look to the deeds and the core of the person, rather than to outer appearances and words. This king captured a thief who belonged to a gang of highwaymen, which was such a source of disruption that no one in the kingdom felt he or his money were safe. Security men, secret police, and soldiers had exerted every effort to catch these murderers and thieves, but to no avail.

When this thief was finally captured, the king himself questioned him, putting him to the worst kind of torture to try and make him tell about the hiding place of his companions. But the king had no success. The more he tortured the thief, the more the thief remained silent and determined not to give away his companions. When the king realized that cruelty would not make the thief reveal his secrets, he changed his method and tried a gentler approach. The king went to the thief and said, "Your body and your soul

are in my hands. I can do whatever I wish with you. I'm telling you that there is no way that you can avoid the jaws of death and pain. The only way out is for you to confess and give me all the information I want. So be wise and accept my proposal. I will give you my solemn promise, the word of a king, that I will forgive you and give you back your freedom."

The thief answered, "O my King, you are striking at a cold iron bar. If you want this information you will have to seek it from a different source, for this tree will bear no fruit for you."

The king said, "All right, if that is the way it is. You are now talking nonsense. I will give you a day to think things over. Be careful that you look into the matter thoroughly. Think of your own welfare and the welfare of the country."

After the king left him, the thief remained alone in his cell in deep thought. Finally, he said to himself, "Why don't I invent some false information? I will give him the name of a place that doesn't exist, so I will have one or two days of peace before the king's soldiers discover my trick." The thief was pleased with this ideal and called for the king, saying, "O my King, I have studied your proposal and have decided to tell you everything I know. So, my King, you should know that the gang gathers every day before the sun rises in a cave that stands on the north side of an olive field that is to the west of the town. The place is marked by an old dry well by the side of the road."

The king replied, "Good for you. You have done well. I will send my soldiers to look for this place. If you are honest, I will let you free, but if you are lying, then death will be your fate."

The king left, and the thief slept with the assurance that no one would come and wake him during the night. Two days passed, and on the third day the door of his cell was opened. The chief guard entered and awakened the thief to say, "Come on, prepare yourself for a breath of freedom. The king has issued an order to set you free, as he promised for the information you gave to him."

The thief, dazed and walking as if he were still asleep, followed the footsteps of the guard as he opened the door of the prison. He was

puzzled how it had happened that the story he had invented had turned into something real and true. Days passed with the thief still bewildered and wandering around lost in thought. When he was about to go mad from too much thinking, he went to an old saint who possessed great stores of knowledge and told him exactly what had happened. The saintly man said, "God has touched your mouth to save your life. Don't deny God's hand. Go and save yourself!"

When the thief heard the saintly man answer in this way, he got up and went to say goodbye to his family, relatives, and tribe. He climbed up a mountain and built a hut for himself on its summit. He spent his days praying and became a hermit saint with a holy power that helped him perform miracles and other wonders.

So, God is Almighty, and it is only He who can turn a thief into a saint.

Thus ends the story, with its share of grief and glory!

The Story of Luck and Fate

ONCE UPON A TIME, there was a man who wanted to know his future. He spent all his time trying to find someone who would foretell his future and tell him of his Luck and Fate. One night while he was sleeping, a voice called to him in his dreams saying, "Get up and go to the laurel woods! There you will find your Luck and Fate." Without hesitation the man got up to answer this call from his sleep. He prepared himself for the journey, impatient to take the road that led to the laurel woods where he would find his Luck and meet his Fate.

Just as he was starting down the road, he saw a beautiful woman standing at the door of an immense palace. When he came near her, she called out, "Welcome to you, my new husband." He answered, "But I'm not your husband, madam." She answered, "Yes, yes, I know that, but I already know you are to become my husband." The man said, "But how is that?" The woman responded, "You see, my lord, I am a widow whose late husband left me a huge palace and these immense gardens, parks, and fields. He also left me flocks of sheep, cows, and goats, for my late husband, bless his soul, loved me very much. Being afraid to leave me alone, he made me promise to go on the first

day after the period of mourning was over, and marry the first man who passed by, and you are the first man to pass."

The man replied "I am sorry ma'am. I cannot put your husband's wish into action because I have been promised that I will meet my Luck and Fate in the laurel woods." The woman said, "Will your Luck and Fate be better than what I am proposing?" He answered, "I don't know, but this is my Luck and Fate," and he went on his journey.

On the way, he met a bold old man with a wrinkled face, deep-set eyes, and veined hands standing at the opening of a mine, who said, "Welcome my only heir!" The man replied, "But I'm not your heir, sir!" Whereupon the man said, "Yes, yes you are. I say this because I already know you will be my heir." The man asked, "How can that be?" and the old man replied, "Look, my son, I am a rich man, richer than Qarun with a wealth that cannot be counted. I possess this gold mine which brings millions and millions, and because I'm near death without a son I went to ask a seer to tell me what to do with all my wealth. He said I should give my wealth to the first man who passes by my gold mine, and you are the first one to pass."

The man answered, "I'm sorry I cannot follow the instructions of your seer, because I have been promised that I will find my Luck and Fate in the laurel woods." The old man asked, "Can your Luck and Fate be better than what I am proposing?" The man said, "I don't know, but this is my Luck and Fate."

He continued on his journey. He saw a priest in simple dress with a shaved head, an open face, and a vague look in his eyes, standing at the door of the monastery. As the man approached the priest, he stopped him, and said, "Welcome, O Saint." The man said, "But I am no saint, sir!" The priest said, "Yes, yes you are! I say this because I know you will become a saint!" The man said, "How do you know that?" The priest replied, "Look, my brother, we are priests here who have dedicated ourselves to prayer and worship and to the welfare of God's children. Last night the elder priest had a vision in which he was told to call the first man who passed by our monastery to become a priest. This person is to have a great place in the kingdom of God, and you are the

first to pass." The man answered, "I am sorry, my brother, I cannot answer the call of your vision because I have been promised that I will meet my Luck and Fate in the laurel woods." The priest asked, "Would your Luck and Fate be better that what I propose to you?" I don't know, my brother, but this is my Luck and Fate."

He went on his way and saw a large group of ministers, noble men, officers, and ordinary people standing at the door of a huge city. As he passed them, they stopped him and said, "Welcome, our mighty King," The man said, "But I am not a king." The grand Vizier said, "Yes, yes, we know you are not. We are saying this because we know you are going to become our king." "How do you know that?" The Grand Vizier replied, "You are in luck, my lord, I am the Grand Vizier in this great kingdom, and as our king died without leaving an heir to the throne he made us promise to go out on the third day after his death and choose for the throne the first man who passes by the gate of the city, and you are the first to pass." The man said, "I am sorry I can't fulfill the wish of your dead king who now sleeps peacefully, because I have been promised that I will meet my Luck and Fate in the laurel woods." "Would your Fate and Luck be better than what I am proposing to you?" "I don't know, sir, but it is my Luck and Fate."

The man went on his journey until he came to the woods. No sooner had he entered the woods than he met a black panther, roaring and snarling. When the man saw the black panther coming towards him, he was shaken with fear and terror and tried to turn and run away. At that moment, by God's will, the panther said to the man, "Where are you going?" The man said, "I'm coming to find my Luck and Fate." The panther said, "Then why are you running away?" The man said, "Because I'm afraid you might eat me." The panther said, "But I am your Luck and Fate." The man answered, "Goodbye, then, I have no wish to meet or see you. I prefer not to have knowledge of my future and would rather return to one of the proposals I received on the way here." The black panther said, "What you have missed is gone. There is no escape from what is written." And with these words, he jumped on him and ate him.

None of you should too quickly say I reject this or that, because your Luck and Fate will catch up with you, even if they take the form of a black panther.

Thus ends the story, with its share of grief and glory!

Part Two
Tales and Episodes of Aleppo

The Tale of the Girl and the Judge

ONCE UPON A TIME a little girl was sweeping happily under the bed and the straw mat when she found a penny. She went to the store and bought some molasses that she hid in a niche above the door. Then, she went about her business awhile until she became hungry enough to eat some of the molasses. It immediately made her feel energetic and full of youthful spirits.

A crow came and snatched the rest up and took it to the forest to eat. When the girl came back from a walk, she found out what happened and became very angry. Sizzling like a fire over coals, she ran after the renegade thief to take her revenge. She followed after him, to see where he would go so she could lay an ambush for him. When he passed by, she caught him, and before he had time to escape she cut off his tail as a punishment for his crime. When the crow looked back and saw that his tail was cut off and some feathers missing, in desperation he became furious and suddenly attacked the little girl, plucking out her eyes and making her totally confused.

The girl went away crying and upset because he had gotten the best of her. In her sorrow she went to complain to the town judge about the severe treatment she had had from the crow.

</ant

She said, "Your Honor, I am only a little girl."

The judge answered, "That's the way God made you. You shouldn't complain about what God has created."

The girl continued, "I was happily sweeping under the bed and the straw mat."

The judge replied, "Cleaning doesn't count as an act of charity, however. You cleaned for your own sake; cleaning is an act of faith."

The girl said, "I found a penny."

The judge said to her, "You were lucky and benefited from your act."

The girl said, "Then I bought some molasses."

The judge said to her, "You enjoyed eating it. Bon appetite!"

The girl said to him, "I took it and hid it in the niche above the door."

The judge said, "You anticipated eating it and felt very happy."

The girl said, "I went about my business until I became hungry enough to eat some of it. It made me feel energetic and full of youthful spirit."

The judge said to her, "You were pleased and suffered no hardship."

The girl said to him, "The crow came and snatched up the rest and took it to the forest to eat."

The judge said, "He was flying around hungry. When he saw the opportunity and no obstacle preventing him, he seized it and ate it. If he hadn't eaten it he would have died."

The girl said to him, "When I came back from my walk, I found out about it and became sizzlingly angry like a fire over coals. I followed after him to take my revenge. I ambushed him, caught him, and cut off his tail before he could escape to punish him for his crime. He turned on me indignantly and plucked out my eyes so I can't see any more."

Infuriated, the judge drew back from the girl and said, "There is no excuse for so many arguments. You are even, and in this evenness there is justice."

The girl was outraged and could scarcely calm herself. She walked away sulking, saying, "Your Honor, no one is satisfied with your judgement. If this is the extent of your wisdom, then the very hair of your beard is wasted, since for everything said you have an answer. Your place—you ignorant judge, you hard-hearted unjust one, you dreamer lacking in wisdom—your place should be at the door of the court rather than on the bench."

Try not to be hard-hearted if you become judges and make sure you do not deviate from what is right if you are appointed governors, but seek true facts and justice, and value duty. Be fair and do not oppress. Acquire knowledge of the case so you can provide a conclusive verdict. Because it is with justice, not by the yoke, and with knowledge, not by ignorance, that we find salvation and keep ourselves from evil. Ignore injuries and prejudices and strive to achieve the welfare of all people.

So that is the tale's ending, did you find it charming or offending?

The Tale of the Three Mice

ONCE UPON A TIME, there were three mice on their way to the public bath, when they met the infamous cat. He circled around them, bringing them to a standstill and saying, "Come let me eat you, you sweet morsels."

The mice were very frightened but remained calm and answered him as if they were not afraid, "Lord Cat, you who are richer than Qarun and all powerful, we fear for your health if you eat us when we are so filthy. Wait until we come out clean from the bath and then eat us, so you won't be in danger of catching any diseases."

The cat said, "You are right. Go get clean and I'll wait for you here by the door."

The mice ran away as if waking from a bad dream and escaping a nightmare, scarcely believing that they had gotten rid of the cat so easily.

They quickly ran into the bath and began to search its many chambers until they discovered three of the best hiding places available. The first went down a well without another thought. The second jumped

into the fountain and remained motionless. The third crawled inside the drain and, like her sisters, was safe until it came time to come out.

The cat waited hour after hour without seeing a trace of the mice until it became dark and the shops closed down. Fearful that he had lost his opportunity, he entered the bath. There, he sniffed around until he discovered what had happened and understood how the mice had tricked him so easily.

Outraged, he paced back and forth until finally he came to the well, demanding, "O mouse of the well, come out so I can eat you!"

The mouse in the well answered clearly, "Go away! I hope you get clobbered on the head. If you had any brains you wouldn't have let a mouse hide in the well."

The cat was sad but stubborn and, in his frustration, beat his cheeks with his paws,[1] and threw himself against the wall. He cried and cried, muttering to himself that perhaps it was his fault. Eventually, he got up and went over to the fountain and leaned over its basin of water, saying, "O mouse of the fountain, come out so I can eat you."

The mouse in the fountain answered fearlessly, "Go away! I hope someone kicks you in your chattering teeth. If you had a brain in your head, you wouldn't have let a mouse hide in a fountain."

The cat was sad but stubborn and, in his frustration, scratched his face with his claws and shredded his skin with his teeth. He cried and cried, muttering to himself that perhaps it was his fault.

Eventually he got up and went over to the drain, saying, "O mouse of the drain, O mouse of the drain, come out so I can eat you."

The mouse of the drain answered in a sassy voice, "Go away! I hope someone knocks you on your wobbly bones. If there were a brain in your head, you wouldn't have let a mouse hide in the drain."

The cat became sad but was still stubborn and, in his frustration, threw himself down, breaking his bones and injuring his head. And the quantity of blood that flowed from him was more than from a mortally wounded person or from a wholesale massacre. He cried out, "Mouse, O mouse, O smallest of small, you put the cat to shame, triumphing over the Greatest of the Great, even though you are only a mouse.

How could this happen?" He cried and complained until he was completely dejected and his voice was fading.

When the mice heard his voice grow weaker and they were sure he was near death, each one came out of his hiding place, drying his hair as he came. Without a worry in the world, they came laughing and singing, "O Cat, O Cat, O monster of the century. You've lived so long, yet are still tempted by evil, crazy about yourself, yet still a cat. How can that be?"

As soon as the cat saw the mice rejoicing at his misfortune, he wanted to get up and attack them, but his eyes rolled back in his head and his body had no strength left. He stretched out once, turned over, and died.

The mice grasped the cat by his paws and swung him around chanting,

Joy, joy, the cat is dead; his eyes like olives, a lemon his head;
His tongue it stinks, come mice and strew it with cumin.
Joy, joy the evil has fled; joy the cat is dead,
O mice, O mice tell the good news to the neighbors,
The cat is dead and done, play mice, have fun.

It often happens that something little and seemingly insignificant overcomes what is big, for in the world there are many such giants who will always remain small. Be warned that all of this really happened and that you must learn from it to accept what is good and reject what is bad!

So that is the tale's ending, did you find it charming or offending?

[1] A sign of strong feeling. Women who mourn the dead use this gesture.

The Tale[1] of our Lady Namlush[2]

WHEN NAMLUSH FINISHED her house work, she went to her spinning wheel to spin and, while she was tugging the material onto the frame, the needle fell from her hand into the fire. Namlush started to cry, saying: "O how terrible, the night is long. To whom can I complain about my misfortune?"

She remained in this state of doom and gloom until her husband Barghuth al-Baraghut,[3] a really quick and diligent fellow, arrived. He greeted her and kissed her tenderly. When he noticed that she was distracted and showing signs of uneasiness and anxiety, he asked: "What happened? What catastrophe has befallen my pretty one?"

Crying, Namlush raised her complaint with him, and after she was finished he embraced her and patted her cheek, saying: "Don't worry. This is a simple matter, easy to resolve. You shouldn't be sad over something that is so easy to fix." With these words, he descended into the fire to get the needle and was burnt to a crisp.

Namlush was sad, sorry, and mad. She tore at her hair and cried until tears poured down her face. She sat at the threshold of her house, full of remorse over what had happened.

At that moment a crow passed by and said, "What has happened to our Lady Namlush that her hair is all disheveled?"

She answered, "Your Lady Namlush's hair is all disheveled due to the death of Zikri, the prince, son of Tibri, who descended into the fire to get a needle and was burnt to a crisp."

The crow became sad, sorry and mad, and refused to croak. The tree saw him and asked, "What has happened to the crow, Saktrun,[4] to make him silent?"

He said, "The crow is silent and our Lady Namlush's hair is disheveled, because they are saddened by the death of Zikri, the prince, son of Tibri, who descended into the fire for a needle and was burnt to a crisp."

The tree was sorry, sad and mad, and dropped all her leaves. The river saw her and asked, "What has happened to the tree, Aryun?"[5]

She said, "The tree is naked, the crow is silent, and our Lady Namlush is disheveled because they are saddened by the death of Zikri, the prince, son of Tibri, who descended into the fire to get a needle and was burnt to a crisp."

The river became sad and sorry and mad, and his water became murky. The goat saw him and asked, "What is the matter with the river, Akrun?"[6]

He answered, "The river is murky, the tree is naked, the crow is silent, and our Lady Namlush's hair is disheveled because they are saddened by the death of Zikri, the Prince, son of Tibri, who descended into the fire to get a needle and was burnt to a crisp."

The goat was sad, sorry and mad, and broke her horns. The shepherd saw her and asked, "Why doesn't the goat, Bila Qurn,[7] have horns?" She said, "The goat is without horns, the river is murky, the tree is naked, the crow is silent, and our Lady Namlush's hair is disheveled because they are saddened by the death of Zikri, the prince, son of Tibri, who descended into the fire to get a needle and was burnt to a crisp."

The shepherd was sad, sorry and mad, and in his fury tore his clothes to shreds. His wife, who was holding a dish of beans for lunch, saw him

and asked, "What is the matter with my husband, Mumaziqun,[8] that he tears his clothes to shreds."

He answered, "Your husband's clothes are torn to shreds, the goat is without horns, the river is murky, the tree is naked, the crow is silent, and our Lady Namlush's hair is disheveled because they are saddened by the death of Zikri, the prince, son of Tibri, who descended into the fire to get a needle and was burnt to a crisp."

The wife was sad, sorry and mad, and turned the dish upside down all over herself. Her daughter, who was embroidering with a long needle, asked, "What is the matter with my mother, Bil Makhlatun,[9] that she is covered with beans?"

She answered, "Your mother is covered with beans, your father has his clothes torn to shreds, the goat has no horns, the river is murky, the tree is naked, the crow is silent, and our Lady Namlush's hair is disheveled because they are saddened by the death of Zikri, the prince, son of Tibri, who descended into the fire to get a needle and was burnt to a crisp."

The daughter was sorry, sad, and really got mad! She stuck the needle in her eye and gouged it out. Her husband saw her like that and asked, "What is the matter with my wife, Bila 'Ayun?"[10]

She answered, "Your wife is without an eye, her mother is covered with beans, her father has his clothes torn to shreds, the goat has no horns, the river is murky, the tree is naked, the crow is silent, and our Lady Namlush's hair is disheveled because they are saddened by the death of Zikri, the prince, son of Tibri, who descended into the fire to get a needle and was burnt to a crisp."

The husband asked, "Is it because of this insignificant problem that all these catastrophes have happened? It isn't wise to make such a mountain out of a molehill. Leave it to me, this is an easy problem to solve. It's foolish to be saddened by such an easy thing to fix."

He rose saying, "I'll take care of this matter in no time." Then he went and caught a flea and married him to Namlush, wishing them a long and happy life. Namlush became happy and arranged her hair with a flower in it and went to sit at the threshold of her house, as radiant as a lamp. When the crow saw Namlush's hair decked with

flowers, he became overjoyed and started to play and sing and was no longer silent.

When the tree saw that the crow was happy again, she too became overjoyed and opened up new leaves and was no longer naked. When the river noticed the tree in bloom and decorated by the prettiest fruit, he became happy and put aside his gloom so that he was no longer murky. When the goat saw that the water of the river again ran clear and pure, she was overjoyed and grew a new set of horns so she was no longer without them.

When the shepherd saw that the goat had new horns, he became happy and took off his old tattered clothes and put on new elegant ones. When the mother saw her husband, the shepherd, coming with his most beautiful clothes, she became happy and bathed herself until she came out as clean and white as the down on a dove.

And no one suffered from the adversity and misfortune of his or her situation except the foolish daughter, who lost an eye and remained one-eyed.

If you grieve, do it sensibly, and if you are happy over something, do it sensibly too. Whatever you do, do it rationally and sensibly, because bad consequences are the result of bad thinking. Therefore, behave reasonably so that your distress can be easily overcome. Do what you can to see that the expression of your happiness won't offend others. Work to maintain good relationships among all people.

So that is the tale's ending, did you find it charming or offending?

[1] This tale is not in verse in Arabic, but a number of the characters' names rhyme, and certain passages have a rhythm that makes them seem more poetry than prose.

² The name Namlush is derived from the word for ant in Arabic.
³ The husband's name means "flea of the fleas."
⁴ The crow's name means "silent."
⁵ The tree's name means "naked."
⁶ The river's name means "murky."
⁷ The name means "without horns."
⁸ His name means "torn to shreds."
⁹ Her name means "covered with beans."
¹⁰ Her name means "without an eye."

The Tale of the Pigeon
and the Crow

ONCE UPON A TIME, a pigeon and a crow were fighting at the door of the alley. Each claimed he came first and insisted the he would not move from the place.

Since birds do not respond to flattery like human beings, the first started saying, "Your cawing is the symbol of monstrosity, while my cooing is the symbol of peace."

The crow answered, "Absolutely not. We birds will never be safe as long as human beings hold the reins of power and kill us, throwing our feathers and bones in the garbage pit.

The pigeon said, "What an ugly black color you have, like the color of soot! My color is the color of peace."

The crow answered, "O pigeon, be open-minded. You cannot judge people by their color or by their appearance, but by what they say and do."

The pigeon responded, "Your meat is inedible!"

The crow answered, "This protects me from the evil of hunters."

The pigeon answered, "Your appearance is repulsive."

The crow answered, "You say this because you are jealous, envious, and cunning."

The pigeon answered, "You thief of soap! It's your character to inflict harm."

The crow answered, "You weak and feeble creature, you shy away from harm and submit to annoyance—not because you are good but because you lack strength."

The pigeon responded, "Beware of the power of the weak, for it is more potent than poison."

The crow said, "It is better if we can agree peaceably. Come, let us talk things over calmly. Let us negotiate how to compromise over this doorstep."

The pigeon said, "There can be no negotiation over the door of the beloved. Prestige comes before anything else and for the sake of right, love, logic, and fairness. The price is cheap."

The crow answered, "Character comes before anything else, so be open-minded and accept what is. Take what I have offered you, since an eye cannot fight a knife, and the victory of the weak over the powerful occurs only as a miracle."

The pigeon said, "O crow, you are good for nothing but frightening and annoying. O bitter, ill-mannered one, you are the source of lying and hypocrisy." And she leapt at him to peck him and cried as if her wing were about to be torn off.

The owl was awakened from his sleep, and, disturbed, he said, "Why is there a war taking place between the pigeon and the crow?"

The pigeon said, "I don't advocate war because war is ugly. We pigeons are all apostles of peace. But if talking is not enough, how without war and killing can a weak person achieve his due?"

The crow said, "I don't advocate war because war is ugly. We crows, all of us, like tranquility and security. But if tension develops, how without war and the spilling of blood can you settle important matters? I was the first to alight at this door, but this pigeon came and called me a liar."

The pigeon said, "Show me proof of what you say."

The crow answered, "Here is a piece of my claw on the door."

The pigeon answered, "O wicked, spiteful one." And she charged at him, wanting to pluck out his feathers and strangle him to end his life.

The owl interfered and said, "Put war aside and don't fight. War only brings destruction. Go sit on the branch of that tree, and when you see me throw a stone, fly over here and whoever gets here first is the rightful winner."

They went and waited on the branch of the tree. When they saw the owl throw the stone, they raced to the doorway. But when they arrived there, they found that it was already occupied by several owls. Then, since the owl and the crow were friends, they agreed to share the door. No one was left out but the pigeon who with great seriousness is still looking for justice and prestige, and waiting for the occupants of the alley to help her evict the owl and the crow.

Take care to follow the example of the owl and the crow, since their way does not lead to destruction. Make yourself sufficiently strong for any occasion, since strength is peace. Right backed by power is accepted as the noble authority.

So that is the tale's ending, did you find it charming or offending?

The Tale of the Cat and Dog

THERE WAS A CLEVER, energetic cat who could cross the street with one leap. She went to the vizier's house where they bathed her, combed her hair, and perfumed her. She went to the prince's house where he dressed her in silk. She went to the sultan's house where he draped her in a cloak decorated in pearls and coral. She went to the king's palace where the King said, "How pretty you are!" And he called his housekeeper to adorn her with earrings, a necklace, a ring, an anklet and a bracelet. When she climbed to the citadel, they lit a candle for her. She extended her paw into a small window, and when she drew it out again it was decorated with henna and endowed with a great strength. She lifted her eyes to God, and they were lined with kohl and all-seeing so that she immediately knew her way.

Her lazy friend, the dog, who spent all his time playing, saw her and asked, "What has happened to you? You have changed so much! You look beautiful and rich."

So the cat told him the whole story saying "I went to the vizier's house, and they bathed me, combed my hair and perfumed me. I went to the prince's house where he dressed me in silk. Then, I went to the sultan's house where he draped me in a cloak decorated with pearls

71

and coral. Next, I went to the king, who said how pretty I was, and then called his housekeeper to adorn me with earrings, a necklace, a ring, an anklet, and a bracelet. When I climbed up to the citadel, they lit a candle for me. When I extended my paw into a window and withdrew it again, it was decorated with henna and endowed with great strength. When I lifted my eyes to God, they became lined with kohl and all-seeing, so I knew my way."

The dog said to himself, "Why should I remain miserable? Why don't I do what the cat has done and seek a high position in life?" So he went to the vizier's house where they locked him up, beat him and finally threw him out. He went to the Prince's house where they locked him up, beat him, and finally threw him out. He went to the sultan's house where they locked him up, beat him, and finally threw him out. He went to the king's palace where they locked him up, beat him, and finally threw him out. When he lifted his eyes to God, he lost his sight and no longer knew his way. When he reached his paw into the window, he stumbled and fell into the abyss and died and was immediately wrapped in seven layers of cloth.

That is the story of the lazy dog, who didn't satisfy his desire for the good life. The one who works hard reaps the rewards of his labor, while the lazy person only reaps disappointment and dejection.

So that is the tale's ending, did you find it charming or offending?

The Episode of
the Spilled Molasses

I HAVE HEARD THIS tale from Taq bin al-Tarantaq who heard it from a crow who was standing at the entrance of the alley with a peach pit in his beak, crowing, "Caw, caw" all the while. As I pulled his tail, he said, "O People of Good Character, may the truth protect you from poverty and destitution."

Once upon a time in an unknown place, there were two sisters. One was rich but small, ugly, and repulsive in appearance, and the other tall, pretty, and of pleasant character but extremely poor. The first sister used to spend as much money as she wanted without a worry, while the second one restrained herself so she could manage to meet the needs of her children and household. One day, while the poor sister was lifting up an earthenware jug of water to clean the straw mat, she found a coin. She thanked God and went to the perfumer's store to buy some molasses. On her way, she met a young man whose hair was unkempt and his clothes ragged, and whose thin, small-boned body showed signs of pain. His face was pale as though he had just come from the dead or was at least on the verge of leaving this life. He said:

> Throw away your molasses and carry me;
> take me to your house; cook food and
> feed me; spread out a mattress for me

so I may sleep; then take a club
and beat me.

The poor sister answered in a respectful tone of voice. "Leave me alone, O best of men, because I do not have time to be cheerful or happy. Complaining is a shortcoming, but what can a destitute person do? Sir, let me go because I can do nothing for you. My children are waiting impatiently for me at home, and if I don't take this molasses to them, they will die of hunger."

The young man didn't seem to care that her eyes filled with tears as he repeated his request again and again. It was as if he were deaf to her words. He said:

Throw away your molasses and carry me;
take me to your home; cook food and feed me;
spread out a mattress for me, so
I may sleep; then take a club and beat me.

When the poor sister could find no way to get rid of him, or no trick so she could slip away from him, she felt like a prisoner and said, "His command belongs to the one who has the power. I truly hope my patience can withstand the force of his demands so I will not complain even though I wish I were dead." Then she poured out the molasses and carried him to her house. She cooked and fed him and lay out a mattress for him to sleep on. Then she took a club and beat him.

In the early morning as the cock crowed, the poor sister rose eagerly to see if there was enough light so she could start her house work. She noticed that the young man had left, so she entered the room. She found the mattress filled with precious gems and gold, and she was filled with joy, saying: "Now my problems are over, and relief is here. Thanks be to God, who is all powerful. Thanks be to Him for this angel that was sent from heaven to save me from my misery!"

Since the poor have rights and are entitled to the money of the rich, and since it is the duty of those who sleep on silk not to forget those who slept with them before on straw mats, she bought a huge palace

and invited every poor man and woman, saying: "Come, eat and drink and be merry. Live here in comfort. There is no reason for you not to have everything you need now that we are successful and no longer destitute or in need. Don't worry any more, but also don't take advantage and be greedy, or careless, or violent. Live in equality because equality brings peace that removes all sense of pain. And remember that the one who makes you aware of his need is not unjust."

A short period of time passed, and the name and reputation of that great palace became known throughout the world. The poor sister became a famous woman. When the older, wealthy sister, the one who spent so much on herself but was still stingy toward others, heard the news of her poor sister's affluence, after all the hardship she had experienced, she became blind with jealousy and envy. She was filled with hatred and spite instead of happiness and gratitude, and said, "I should be the only wealthy one. How can my sister become rich? I am the only famous one. How can my sister become famous and make people grateful to her? Even though I am rich, I like to receive presents. Certainly, now that my sister has such an easy life, she would like the same thing. I will take her a gift that will make her feel closer to me, and that way I can find out what the secret of her success is. Maybe, with this present and some smooth talking I will be able to get information on the method and way to obtain that treasure I dream about, and I will become lucky like she is."

She went to her sister's house and entered as if it were her own, saying: "O my sister, who used to lie together with me in the same bed. For the sake of my love for you and my happiness for you, please tell me the secret of your luck."

The sister who had been poor before told her the story in detail, but before she finished the jealous sister thanked her for the information and flew out the door. She entered her own house like a cat and threw a coin near the earthenware jug. Then she put on the maid's dress so she would appear poor and pretended to sweep the straw mat. She picked up the coin and thanked God and went to the perfumer's store to buy molasses. But when she had almost reached home and no young man had stopped her, she retraced her footsteps to search for a young

man with the characteristics her sister had described. She stopped one
and said to him:

> Tell me: Throw away your molasses and carry me;
> take me to your house; cook food and feed me;
> spread out a mattress for me so I may sleep;
> then take a club and beat me.

The young man said in an angry voice, "How dare you! Leave me
alone, woman! I do not have time to play games or be happy! Com-
plaining is a shortcoming, but what can a destitute person do? Ma-
dame, let me go because I can do nothing for you. My children are
waiting impatiently for me at home, and if I don't hurry and join them
they will die of hunger."

The envious, jealous sister didn't pay any attention to him or care
that his eyes were filled with tears. She angrily repeated her request
several times saying:

> Tell me: Throw away your molasses and carry me;
> take me to your home; cook food and feed me;
> spread out a mattress for me so I may sleep;
> then take a club and beat me.

When the young man could find no way to get rid of her or no way
to slip away from her, he felt perplexed and said: "I ask God to give me
patience. If you want to force me to say it, then I'll do it." He said:

> Throw away your molasses and carry me; take me
> to your home; cook food and feed me; spread out
> a mattress for me so I may sleep;
> then take a club and beat me.

The rich and jealous woman became very happy as she dreamed
about the treasure she would obtain, as if she had already won the

victory after a long period of waiting. So she poured out the molasses and carried him to her house. She cooked for him and fed him and lay out a mattress for him to sleep on. Then she took a club and beat him.

Next morning, the jealous, envious sister got up, anxious and greedy, and entered the room, anticipating all the precious gems and gold. But all she found was the mattress soaked in urine and shit. She had hit him so hard that he had become weak and ill and his nerves undone, so that what happened occurred without his being aware of what he had done.

Take a lesson from this story and beware of envy and jealousy. Don't enter the door of stinginess, because though it may seem desirable at first, in the end it is narrow like the neck of a funnel. Be generous in deed as well as in word. Don't seek after beauty, goods, and money but instead after truth, justice, and good works. Poverty is not to be despised nor should wealth necessarily engender respect, and ugliness is not shameful nor beauty the only quality to be admired.

Thus the episode ends with all its events, was it unclear or did it make sense?

The Tale of the Little Bitty Thing

Once upon a time, there was a little bitty thing that flew up and sat on a wall where everyone could see him. Finding a bit of string there, he wiped his rear end and flung it down at the neighbors saying:

Hurry, wash this dirty string for me
My uncle's on the way, you see
With a dog that wants a bone to eat
But the bone's still on the butcher's meat
And the butcher now has run away
Throw open the doors; call a holiday
Let Aleppo be happy at what he brought
Not robbery but fair prices for all they bought.

A bottle and an apple for me
A bottle and an apple for you
And to anyone who comes
And to anyone who goes
To anyone who is present
To anyone who is absent
Who goes on a trip
Or who comes from a trip
A bottle and an apple from this garden
The rotten one and the bird-pecked one
Out the door on the garbage will go
And this fine share belongs to the crow.

A greedy girl happened upon the shiny bottle and the dew-bespangled apple. She gathered them up and concealed them under her dress, until she could hide them in a jug under the bed in her room. The crow flew back from the forest and around the square. When he saw neither bottle nor apple, he became furious and started rushing around and hollering as if he were being slaughtered,

Where, where is the one with my share?
Say, say, how I'll find the way! Thief, thief may
You come to grief. Where, where is the thief with my share?

A listening snake beckoned him to come and led him to the greedy one's house. The crow cried, "Despair, despair to the one with my share!"

The greedy girl answered, "Ask the peddlers, why should I care? Don't yell at me, it's not my affair!"

The crow answered,

Uncouth, uncouth, nothing but untruth
Stealing, stealing, you're so unfeeling
Useless all that lying, better stop denying
Prepare for grief, you greedy thief!

And then the crow pecked at her with his beak, and plucked her up in his claws to fly higher and higher. After thinking awhile he asked her, "How big is the earth, spiteful one?"

She answered, "As big as a jug or smaller."

The crow said, "O perfidious one, then I can wait. You unfeeling, greedy one. It's not too late!"

He flew higher and higher with her. Then he asked, "How big is the earth now, spiteful one?"

The greedy one answered, "As big as a plate or smaller."

The crow replied "O source of all problems, then I can wait. You of worthless origins, it's not too late."

The crow flew higher and higher and then asked her, "How big is the earth now, spiteful one?"

The greedy one answered, "As big as a button or smaller."

The crow said "O you with evil face, then I can wait. You without shame, it's not too late."

And he flew higher and higher with her. Then he asked, "How big is the earth, spiteful one?"

The greedy one answered, "As big as the head of a pin or smaller."

The crow replied "You inspirer of nightmares, I can wait. You gloomy one, it's not too late."

He flew higher and higher with her. Then he asked, "Now, how big is the earth?"

The greedy one answered, "Without length or breadth, neither large nor small. I don't see anything now at all!"

The crow said, "The time is right at this great height. I'll soon avenge with sweet revenge your evil deeds that come from greed!"

He turned and opened his claws, and the greedy one slipped away, falling, falling, falling, tumbling and twisting until she came to a crashing end.

Pay heed to me! Control your passion for things you think you want. Go up to bed now and to your sweet dreams. Talking is over for today, so don't ask for another story at this point, do you hear me? To ask for more is bad for you and can't lead to any useful end. It won't protect you, ultimately, from bitterness and evil. So be content, pursue your ambitions enthusiastically without despair but also without forgetting the lesson this tale teaches.

So that's the tale's ending, did you find it charming or offending?

[1] This tale is mixed in the Arabic version with some parts in rhyme and some parts in prose. The introductory parts are mostly nonsense meant to set the mood. They have little to do with the parts that follow.

The Tale of the Fly

ONCE UPON A TIME, there was a fly buzzing around like the sound of the *rababa*[1] until finally it landed on the wall, saying, "How high, how high you are, O wall, you evil obstacle, good for nothing!"

The wall answered, "How tall am I? How tall am I indeed when a mouse can dig a hole in me?"

The fly flew until it reached the mouse and said, "I'll poke you, I'll poke you, O mouse, you worst enemy of the house."

The mouse replied, "What does it matter if you poke me or not, when what I worry about is that a cat may eat me?"

The fly continued on until it saw the cat and said, "How ferocious you are, O cat Harun, O beast of the centuries!"

The cat Harun answered, "Am I so ferocious when the stick can hit me?"

The fly continued on until it met the stick and said, "I should beat you, beat you, O stick, you punisher of aggressors and rebels."

The stick answered, "How weak I am though when the fire burns me?"

The fly continued on until it met the fire and said, "How hot you are, O fire, consumer of the cold and the cutting edge of the blade."

The fire answered, "Am I so hot when the water extinguishes me?"

The fly flew on its way until it came to water and said, "How power-ful is your ability to extinguish, O water, you who are the disease and cure all at the same time."

The water answered, "Is my extinguishing effect so great when the goat drinks me?"

The fly jumped and landed on the goat and said, "O how well you consume the water, you breaker of branches in the walnut tree."

The goat answered, "Is it any concern how well or how poorly I consume water when the butcher slaughters me?"

The fly flew on until it reached the butcher and said, "How well, O butcher, you know how to slaughter. You lowly swindling knife."

The butcher got upset and angry and said, "You busybody, what does it matter how well I slaughter when a little fly can bother me? You devil, you give me such a headache from putting your nose where it doesn't belong. Here, I will give you what you deserve!" And he struck out at the fly and hit it.

Be careful not to be an unwelcome intruder or to be too curious. Learn that there are priorities so that some things are more important than others.

So that is the tale's ending, did you find it charming or offending?

[1] A one-stringed instrument.

The Episode of the Mother Goat

I HEARD FROM TAQ bin al-Tarintaq about a sheep that hung from a doorway in the alley with a bunch of mint in his mouth, and whenever someone would pull his ear he would say ma-a-a! It is said dear listeners— may justice preserve you from treachery, that in a small stable near the Namir River there once lived a mother goat, Anzat al-Anuz, and her two little ones whom she considered her dearest and most valuable treasures. This mother goat loved her kids so much that she would hang amulets on them to protect against danger from bears, falling into traps, and all other challenges they might meet. Because they occupied such an important place in her heart, she saw to it that they were well-groomed and well-brought-up. She gave them the best education and counseled them to work hard and not loaf around. She instructed them so their minds would grow and they would not be deceived.

Because the baby goats had weak teeth and soft hooves and were not able to cut and chew dry grass or digest animal feed, the mother goat used to graze on the most tender grass to make the best milk for them. One morning, after the baby goats had awakened from their nice sleep and pleasant dreams, the mother goat went out into the fields to graze

But because she was afraid the wolf might harm her little ones, she told them before she left: "Don't open the door for anyone but me, my little ones. You will know it is I, my dearest ones, when you see my leg extended under the door. My leg, you know, is white while the wolf's leg is black. I promise not to be too long. So be careful, little ones." Then the mother goat started out on the road that led to the fields.

The wolf, who had been listening from behind the wall, came out. His mouth began to water and he bared his wicked teeth. To carry out his plan, he ran first to the edge of the forest where there were builders working. Slowly and silently, he walked over to dip his black paws in the plaster until they were all white. Then he set off singing, as he thought with glee of how soon he would fill his stomach with fresh goat meat. As he approached the stable, he slowed down so he wouldn't be panting and out of breath. Before the door he stopped and knocked, all the while licking his chops.

The little goats from inside replied with confident voices, "Who is there? If you are good, pray stay, but if you are evil, go away."

The wolf imitated the voice of their mother and answered, "I am your mother, my beloved ones, so open the door."

The little goats answered, "Our mother said not to open the door to anyone but her. If you are our mother show us a sign so we may recognize you."

The wolf extended his paw under the door.

The little goats' faces brightened with happiness and they began to exclaim, "It's her white leg. Our mother is back. O joy, O happiness!"

They jumped quickly to open the door and were surprised when they found themselves facing the treacherous wolf, whose face was beaming with pleasure at the calamity and distress he was causing and whose eyes shone like the coals of a fire. The little goats stood there facing

this treacherous wolf with all his deceptiveness and cruelty, as he stood blocking their way with the saliva dripping from his mouth. They started crying and pleaded with him, but the wolf didn't give them a moment's notice.

He took them to his dwelling, which was full of garbage, and said to them, "This is no time for pleading, be quiet and prepare yourselves for death. Shouting will get you nowhere." He secured them tightly, laughing and dancing as he started the fire.

Then in anticipation of the great event, he began to sing:

> Little goats you are my happiness
> I won't share you with anyone; you are mine.
> I consider you the prize of the hunt
> And the prize of the hunt, you know, is slaughtered
> After it is slaughtered, it is skinned
> After it is skinned, it is cleaned
> After it is cleaned, it is cooked
> And after that it is eaten
> So prepare yourself for the feast
> This evening my beloved
> I promise you on the word of a wolf
> That I won't delay you long while I gather the firewood.

By the time the sun started to go down, the mother goat, Anzat al-Anuz, had finished gathering the grass in bundles and had eaten enough herself to produce a good quantity of milk. She wanted to return to her kids before darkness came with its dangers.

As she approached the door she started to sing to signal her little ones that she had arrived:

> Fog and clouds, clouds and fog
> My children, my beloved
> Open the door for your mother
> In her horns are tender grass
> Her udder contains good milk for

Her beloved kids
Hurry and eat until you are full
Lie down and drink until you have had enough.

She continued along her way singing these happy songs until she
arrived at the stable. But when she knocked on the door, she didn't get
any answer, so she extended her leg under the door. Her face became
pale and she felt that some evil had befallen her kids.

She charged the door, breaking it open, and, when she found no
one there, she was terrified, saying,

I swear it can be no one but the treacherous wolf
He is the only one capable of such an evil deed
But the Almighty is more powerful than such treachery
I must crush the thief and give him what he deserves.

She flew like a wounded eagle and raged like a injured lion, crying
aloud,

I am Anzat al-Anuz al-Anayzia
My horns are of iron and
My hooves of lead
Whoever doesn't believe me
Let him face me
And do battle with me.

She kept on shouting until the wolf's dwelling appeared before her.
She ran up to it and shouted out at the top of her lungs,

Wolf, O Wolf
O Monster of the Underworld
O Hypocrite with no goodness in you
O Evader, show yourself so I can see
That you get what you deserve

Folktales from Syria

Wolf, O Wolf
O Monster of the Underworld

After awhile he showed his ugly face, and when he saw her he quickly ran toward her. When he was face to face with Anzat al-Anuz, he crouched and sprang at her, and the battle began. For a long time Anzat al-Anuz and the wolf were locked in battle to see who would win. She charged with horns; they wrestled; they kicked up the dust of the hills and brought down the dirt of the mountains. They broke the branches of the trees and fought and fought until it was dark. By then the goat, Anzat, was standing firm while the wolf was almost exhausted. Finally, the wolf collapsed with Anzat's horn piercing his chest as a punishment for his treachery.

Anzat al-Anuz won in the end, and with her victory, Justice won, too.

When she saw she had triumphed, Anzat called her little ones to her, those little ones who were more dear to her than treasure. They rushed eagerly to their mother and nestled against her. She embraced them and kissed them tenderly.

Then they all returned to the stable playing drums and cymbals and singing,

> Our home is safe
> The treacherous wolf is dead
> Over every treacherous one
> There is someone more mighty
> Over every powerful one
> There is a most Powerful One.
> With justice, we defend our land
> Our doors, our ceilings, our walls.
> Our home, and the people of
> Our home come first before the neighbors
> But the neighbors come before the building

Home, O home, crown us with laurel
We have erased our shame.

In this way, the little lambs learned the meaning of protection, for no one worries about the rose except the one who plants and waters it, and no one worries about the child except the one who bore and raised him.

Thus the episode ends with all its events, was it unclear or did it make sense?

The Tale of Tata

طاطا يا طاطا

يا ذا الطربوش ويا ذا الحطاطة

صحنان من البطاطا

وكبة مع رغيف

توزع مجانا على رصيف

فقولوا يا لطيف

امرأة سمينة كمؤخرة الدجاجة

نزلت الى المدينة

فكسرت زجاجة

ولكي تتهرب من دفع سعرها

رمت على الاولاد سبب كسرها

فقال الاولاد:

« نحن لسنا بحرامية

ولو اننا من كسرها

لدفعنا ثمنها مية »

فأشعل ضو وأطفىء ضو

وجاء القط فقال: نو نو والاولاد يلعبون

وجاء الكلب فقال: عو عو والاولاد يلعبون

وجاءت العنزة فقالت: ماء ماء والاولاد
يلعبون

وجاءت النعجة وقالت: ماع ماع والاولاد
يلعبون

وجاء الحمار فبدأ بالنهيق والاولاد يلعبون

وجاء الغراب فأخذ بالنعيق والاولاد يلعبون

The Tale of Tata[1]

Tata, Tata, wearing a tarbush and scarf on his head,
Two plates of potatoes and kibbi[2] with bread,
Free on the sidewalk for all to be fed,
"God have mercy upon us!" they said.

A woman with a fat ass like a hen went to the city one day
She broke a bottle but was too cheap to pay
So she blamed some children playing along the way
"If we'd done it we'd have paid," was all they'd say.

A light went on and a light went out.
A cat came by and cried "Meow, Meow," while the children
played,
A dog came by and barked "Bow, Wow," while the children
played,
A goat came by and bleated "Ma, Ma," while the children played,
The sheep came by and bleated "Ba, Ba," while the children
played,
The donkey came by and brayed "Hee, Haw," while the chil-
dren played,
The crow came by and croaked "Caw, Caw," while the chil-
dren played,

The guard came by and blew "Toot, Toot," and when the children heard his horn they all ran home as fast as they could. For the children all know that the guard will believe what the adults say more than what the children say, even when what they say is true.

Take note of this lesson: Animals create a calm atmosphere while humans provoke a sense of fear.

That's the tale's ending, did you find it charming or offending?

[1] This tale appears in partial rhyming verse in Arabic. The introductory verses don't make much sense and serve rather to set the mood. The main purpose of the tale is to teach vocabulary words and animal sounds. The storyline thinly disguises this purpose.

[2] Kibbi is a ground meat and burghul mixture, usually served fried in the shape of a meatball.